Otherworldly Hamlet

Essay Series 10

John O'Meara

Otherworldly Hamlet
Four Essays

Guernica

Montreal, 1991

Typeset and printed in Canada.

Antonio D'Alfonso, publisher-editor
Guernica Editions Inc., P.O. Box 633, Station N.D.G.,
Montreal (Quebec), Canada H1N 2Y5

The Publisher gratefully acknowleges financial support from
Canada Council and Le ministère des Affaires culturelles

Legal Deposit — Second Quarter
Bibliothèque nationale du Québec and National Library of Canada.

Canadian Cataloguing in Publication Data

O'Meara, John, 1953-
(Essay series; 10)
ISBN 0-920717-50-0
1. Shakespeare, William, 1564-1616. Hamlet. I. Title.
II. Series: Essay series (Montréal, Quebec)
PR2807.043 1991   822.3'3   C91-090130-9

Contents

Acknowledgments

Two of these essays have appeared in print before: the essay on 'Sorrow', in *Cahiers Élisabéthains*, Vol. 35, 1989; and the essay on 'Sexuality', in *Hamlet Studies*, Vol.10, 1988.

Of the many who have contributed to the appearance of this volume, I especially wish to thank my great teacher and very dear friend, Joseph Cameron, and all those at Willibrord's who over the years have shared the struggle with him, and especially during the years 1986-1988 when I had the very good fortune of being amongst them. To Theresa Cullen, and to her personal vision of me during that time, I owe more than I can say, and I would also wish to single out Moira Carley who by thoughtfully introducing me, on a small occasion, as 'a Shakespearean', unbeknownst to her rescued me from oblivion. To Antonio D'Alfonso, whose mark on the production of this volume runs deeper than I had latterly conceived, I owe an important debt for his faithfulness over all these years. And I must take the occasion once again to acknowledge Nicholas Brooke who, by his remarkable example, virtually created me, and whose influence is to be found embedded in just about every word of this volume.

John O'Meara

In memory of my father

But that the dread of something after death —
The undiscover'd country, from whose bourn
No traveller returns — puzzles the will....

Preface on Hamlet *and Luther*

One of Luther's editors has shown how in Luther's experience of faith:

> It is confessed that the mystery of God's act in all its priority incorporates and includes the re-direction of man's capacity of decision. Another way of putting this is to say that faith includes infinitely more than the deciding capacity of man.[1]

By the end of Shakespeare's play, Hamlet has undergone an experience of providential re-direction of his destiny which roughly suggests the Lutheran experience of faith.[2] It is fairly obvious, however, that the providential experience is far from being altogether satisfactory to Hamlet and that it *remains* painfully ironical for him to the bitter end. If so, this is precisely because of Hamlet's need to affirm his own 'deciding capacity' in his attempt to relate himself to his otherworldly experience, including his attempt to relate himself to that experience in his commitment to revenge. The standard conventional view of Hamlet as the hero of indecision, a man who suffers because 'he could not make up his mind', pales miserably before the play's evidence of a tremendous affirmation on Hamlet's part that man *should* be able to decide the ultimate question of his destiny, especially since, in Hamlet's case, that destiny depends on an otherworldly experience that continues to elude him.

The contrast with Luther, in fact, is extensive, for Luther himself had *his* otherworldly experience, although he never went so far as to claim that he had actually been visited by a Ghost (though his father had, ironically, suspected that it was the Devil that had spoken to Luther all along). Years later recalling that decisive experience which gave him the new insight on which he was to build his entire mature Reformation faith, Luther said that, at the time he had the experience, he felt that he 'had entered paradise itself through open gates'.[3] His 'tower experience' — so called because it came to him while in the tower of the Augustinian monastery in Wittenberg — had brought to Luther his clearest vision of what 'the righteousness of God' entailed:

> There I began to understand that the righteousness of God is that by which the righteous lives by a gift of God, namely by faith. And this is the meaning: the righteousness of God is revealed by the gospel, namely, the passive righteousness with which merciful God justifies us by faith...[4]

In the tower at Wittenberg, Luther had received ultimate confirmation, as Luther's editor puts it, that:

> In faith, man stands before God in the light of grace. For him, even at his best, there is no other possibility...; aside from this, the actuality of his situation is that he is totally a sinner.[5]

Himself fresh from Wittenberg, Hamlet comes away from *his* 'tower' experience with the Ghost (the encounter takes place in a remote area high

14

up on the battlements of Elsinore castle) with a vision of human nature that, as I show, is fundamentally Lutheran in tendency. In the 'actuality of [their] situation' — in contradistinction from 'the imputation of righteousness'[6] which Hamlet receives from the otherworldly basis of his vision — men and women are, for Hamlet, totally sinners; all are damned in the experience of libido which nothing can cure. It is crucial to note, however, how Hamlet's vision, as Hamlet comes away from the Ghost, is in direction in inverse relation to Luther's tower experience which allowed Luther to admit himself a sinner only because, as revealed to him, there was now no longer any reason for despairing of salvation. Thus, a matter which did not concern Luther because of the thrust of his experience, but which does profoundly concern Hamlet, is the whole basis on which one could know that humankind was universally degenerate. Luther was in the end to elaborate his vision of human degeneracy, in contrast with the divine imputation of righteousness, on the basis of a clear understanding of the gospel fully inspired into him during his tower experience — understanding which directly confirmed his own personal experience. Shakespeare, through Hamlet, raises the question of how the vision of degeneracy *itself* relates to a basis in immediate otherworldly revelation, for it is on the basis of the Ghost's account of himself, and only on that basis as I show, that Hamlet has come to understand that such degeneracy is indeed the case.

Scholars are not convinced that Luther was not in fact mistaken in his account of when the tower experience came to him. This attribution to Luther of a lapse in memory is a potentially dramatic indication that the meaning and value of Luther's experience as revelation were in a sense irrelevant to the vision of human nature that Luther propounded, that vision depending as it did in the end on a clear reading of the gospel. But the meaning of Hamlet's 'tower' experience with the Ghost, and especially its value as visionary objectification, are for Hamlet of the utmost concern. For without what I call the sustaining 'actuality and coherence' of immediate, otherworldly vision, there can be for Hamlet, from the time the Ghost disappears, no full certainty that the view of man and woman that lingers in him from that vision and defines that vision for him, is sufficiently well-founded. Nor, consequently, can Hamlet's view of human degeneracy find a proper focus in relation to the cleansing act of revenge that has been required of him.

The inverted relation to Luther points up a relative emphasis in Shakespeare's presentation that is critical in understanding Shakespeare's own vision in his play. That vision is not simply Lutheran, nor is it at all a simple response to Luther. Luther's vision of humankind's degenerate condition and of the role played by libido in that condition was, I believe, the most significant immediate influence on Shakespeare when Shakespeare was producing his play. From Hamlet's treatment of Gertrude and Ophelia as well as from the way Hamlet looks upon himself, it would seem that Shakespeare in this play takes Luther's negative vision of human libido very seriously indeed. But what of a continued, otherworldly justification for that vision, of no further account to Luther? Hamlet's vision of the degenerate tendency of human libido, otherwise felt so strongly by him to have its basis in a truthful rendering of the human condition, must appear to have implications all the more tragic and grave just because that vision, once the Ghost disappears, for the most part lacks a clear and sustained connexion to its original justification in otherworldly revelation.

One of the effects which Hamlet has in single-handedly seeking to impose his vision on his world is to highlight tragically what would have had to be surrendered to that vision at the time *Hamlet* was written — namely, the innocent, romantic view of love and of religion so characteristically Elizabethan. In fact, the impact of the Lutheran vision of human libido on Shakespeare would not have been nearly so tragic as it was, had Shakespeare, as a product of the Elizabethan age, not been himself so hopelessly romantic. Although I have said that I believe the Lutheran vision of human libido constituted the fresh influence on Shakespeare when he was writing *Hamlet,* a whole number of other influences continued to play into Shakespeare's representation. Another strong influence playing into Shakespeare's representation at this time was the whole disposition towards otherworldly vision stemming, as I show, from a continuous, native tradition going back through Thomas Kyd to Thomas Sackville. As the evidence of that literary tradition suggests — especially the precedent set by Kyd — the question of continuing to base an account of the human condition in a direct otherworldly vision remained, right up to the time of *Hamlet,* a critical consideration. Within this tradition — and *Hamlet* cannot be separated from it — man's capacity for acting ethically at all depended on his being directly sustained by an ideal otherworldly relation. *Severed* from that ideal relation, Hamlet cannot, in fact, properly focus his revenge — otherwise heroically required of him to halt the course of evil in his world — in a manner satisfying 'perfect conscience'. Separation from an otherworldly experience is for Hamlet, as it was for Kyd's hero, Hieronimo, a matter consequently of very special concern and sorrow.

The question of what then becomes possible to Hamlet in his tragically dissociated condition receives further imaginative treatment in the play in the form of Hamlet's extended meditation on the possibilities of revenge implied throughout, of which I attempt a convenient outline in the section on Revenge. Herein we shall find some of the play's most dramatic pictorialized evidence of that identification with the 'deciding capacity of man' which I am claiming simply must follow in Hamlet from the condition that separates him from the otherworldly basis of his vision. Still more evidence of the identification with man's deciding capacity is to be found in the play's last movement which follows on Hamlet's failure to execute his revenge in the prayer scene. Indeed in light of the play's insistent preoccupation with man's deciding capacity, right down to the play's very last sequence, the theme of the impending death of Hamlet, formally announced long before there can be any resolution of the question of vision, must appear to have an effect all the more tragically pathetic. The play's final effect of pathos is underlined for us in an especially striking way with reference to the painting by El Greco which Shakespeare's final action seems almost to invoke directly, but with which Shakespeare's action in the play as a whole, because of its underlying preoccupation with the tragic frustration of Hamlet's vision, must be seen as ultimately contrasting poignantly.

I

Sorrow

When Thomas Kyd preceeded the play's events in *The Spanish Tragedy* with the Ghost of Andrea giving an account of his descent into hell, he was building on an innovation which Thomas Sackville had introduced years before in his contribution to the *Mirror for Magistrates*.[1] When Sackville's *Induction* was first presented to the Mirror's curiously sensitive, though always well-meaning body of distinguished compilers, the poem had roused them to wonder and consternation at the audacity of its invention. Radically unlike the other stories in the *Mirror*, the *Induction* was being made room for as a 'preface' to Sackville's less anomalous contribution of the story of Buckingham; as an artistic *cadre* for that story, Sackville's *Induction* was unusual, for both its elaborate sophistication and audacious use of the vision-structure which the *Mirror* poets had been applying to the stories in the tradition of Boccaccio and Lydgate. Each story in the *Mirror* was narrated by the Ghost of its subject who was to be imagined appearing to the poets in a vision. With only one exception (the ghost of Richard of Gloucester was pictured 'howlinge from the deepe pit of hell'), the ghosts had been imagined by the *Mirror* poets as speaking either freshly dead or on the point of death (and thus as an 'Image of death'), or else 'newly crept out of the grave'. Sackville's *Induction* had disturbed this pattern by setting its speaking ghost amongst thousands of others in the depths of hell, after claiming to have been led into hell on a journey by the Goddess Sorrow.

The fear of the *Mirror* poets was that Sackville's procedure was likely to be ill-taken, since the hell-setting implied a judgment on the statesmen ghosts, whereas it had been until then the general procedure of the *Mirror* poets to refrain cautiously from such judgments. Even worse, in its sympathetic qualities Sackville's judgment 'savoured' of Purgatory, thus catering to the papist misrepresentation of the otherworld. The fretfulness was allayed by the intervention of the *Mirror's* less excitable voices. Falling back on Renaissance syncretic method, it was concluded that Sackville's hell was really no hell at all, but in fact a symbol for the grave; and so it was that Sackville's subversive *Induction* was reconciled to *Mirror* procedure: even then, the syncretic solution was unnecessary since Sackville's Hell was merely 'a Poesie', relevant 'adornment' merely.

The decision of the *Mirror* poets to restrict their visions to the moment of death was not merely to be traced to their determination to eschew political and theological controversy. The extraordinary complacency with which some of the *Mirror* poets treat of the topical implications of the *Induction* show that. The procedure said a great deal rather about their basically rationalist assumptions about the nature and function of the creative imagination. In refraining (with the exception of Richard of Gloucester whose damnableness was obvious to all) from taking their ghosts beyond the brink of the grave, the *Mirror* poets were merely acting on their limited belief as to how far the creative imagination could go in developing a conceit which had in any case been adopted more from deference to tradition than from any real insight into its poetic function. Nor is this implication of *Mirror* procedure contradicted by one or two spectacular exceptions to the rule, most notably in the ghosts of York and Collingbourne who are imagined speaking one out of a headless trunk, the other with his heart in his hand, 'smoking forth the lively spirit'. In these cases, the *Mirror* poets were merely employing a sensationalistic rhetoric guided by a sense of the miraculous reality one might effectively project onto death for compulsive reading; for which the conceit, that is, served merely as conceit without any suggestion of a projection of literal reality. Not only were the ghosts kept scrupulously close to the grave, it was clearly established at first that they were to be regarded as the creations of story-telling: at most, they could receive a sensationalistic representation from the influence of a fantastic ardor always rhetorical in purpose.

The basic procedure for telling the stories finally rationalized the appearance of the ghosts. But, in proceeding along the lines it did, the practice of the *Mirror* poets stood out in sharp contrast against the claim to visionary organization which even the *Mirror* poets themselves acknowledged respectfully of their models,

Boccaccio and Lydgate. This isn't to say, of course, that the *Mirror* poets did not believe in the power of creative imagination; indeed, the effectiveness of their stories depended on it. Thus, it is correct to say, with Alwin Thaler, that 'the *Mirror* group believed in true feigning, true imagining by poet and audience'.[2] It is an account, however, which obscures the actual position of the *Mirror* group for whom 'true feigning' consisted in seeing that 'imagining' was merely an effective means for conveying what was true, and not actually true in itself.

It was inevitable, therefore, that these poets should fail utterly to appreciate the extraordinary status of Sackville's *Induction* as vision. Significantly, the obvious function of Sackville's poem as vision led Baldwin, the *Mirror's* chief editor, to associate it rather with the extraordinary creations of Lydgate and Boccaccio than with the more sensible fictions of the *Mirror* group. Yet far from representing an effort at real understanding, Baldwin's gesture merely served to highlight the group's spectacular incomprehension, for the syncretic-rhetorical reduction showed how Sackville's visionary journey was finally to be taken. Sackville's vision was to be reduced to symbolic thought or to fiction: what the *Mirror* group had failed to see was that the journey Sackville described took reality precisely from the extraordinary developments by which mere thought had transformed itself into vision. The Goddess Sorrow, who serves as Sackville's guide for the journey into Hell, could not have put the import of Sackville's experience more unambiguously:

...behold the thing that thou erewhile
Saw only in thought....

(ll. 530-531).

Sackville's *Induction* stands out from the other more modestly-shaped stories in the *Mirror* by virtue of its active belief in the transformational powers of the imagination. From that belief, it followed that any account of the mind's workings where the fiction appeared to be an outer shell for thought was to be taken in fact as literal vision. In presenting its vision, Sackville's poem drew on the conventional medieval form of the marvellous journey. In doing so, it had taken on the narrative form as literal fact. The power that had made possible the journey was the Goddess-guide Sorrow, who according to the pattern is more than merely a personification. She is the spiritual objectification of the poet's own grief, round whom the expanded vision of hell takes place: the visionary product of a 'busie minde' lost to its metaphorical 'musings' (ll. 64, 156).

In beginning *The Spanish Tragedy* with a descent into hell himself, Kyd could not have been unaware of Sackville's use of the marvellous journey as vision. Whether or not the intensity of the narrative actually justifed the claim to vision is not the point, neither here nor in Sackville. Both accounts, unlike the *Mirror*, acted on the assumption of the literal function of narrative, thus projecting, in contrast to the *Mirror*, an unlimited belief as to how far the imagination could develop the traditional conceit inherited from Boccaccio and Lydgate. In all cases, the conceit of the speaking ghost had been adopted to intensify the impact of the tragic events treated. That much is clear from the use made of the conceit by the *Mirror* poets. The capacity of the audience to imagine a speaking ghost, to lose themselves, as it were, to the fiction, accounted for the intensity with which the stories would be received. By filling out the fiction, the imagination of the audience built on the intensity which the poets likewise had brought to their story-telling by imagining themselves as speaking ghosts. However, the fact that the narrative could also serve, as in Boccaccio, to express a claim to literal vision ('As hym thoughte in the inward siht')[3] could only have added to the psychological value of the narrative for both poet and audience. That value was likely to be intensified the more extraordinary and expansive the vision, so that Sackville and Kyd had everything to gain from linking a vision of the speaking ghost with an evocation of the otherworld, a larger vision of the descent into hell.

The full metaphysical significance of this linkage in Kyd can be best appreciated by first tracing what Sackville had done to Boccaccio. Boccaccio's vision had operated within the tradition of an artistic framework for the narrative of falls, which set the pattern for the later narrative tragedy of the *Mirror*. As Howard Baker points out, in his *Induction to Tragedy*: 'The ordinary procedure was to have the ghosts of the fallen Worthies appear successively as in a vision, before the poet... The ghost... was sometimes conducted from the infernal regions to the poet's chamber to the "stage" by a guide...'.[4] It was Sackville's daring innovation at this time to fix once again on the literal possibilities of the journey in Boccaccio's vision, building in part on the powerful precedent of epic tradition, including Dante, but, primarily, Virgil. The appearance of the ghost before the poet in Boccaccio already assumed a journey from the infernal regions to the poet's chamber. In that journey the ghost had been led by a guide. In his own development of the vision, Sackville had used the guide, inversely, to carry the poet from his chamber on a journey into the infernal regions where ghosts awaited him.

In a further development, Kyd had brought both models together. The drama of the Ghost's appearance in the Prologue ultimately emphasizes his immediate presence in the world: that is where the Ghost finds himself quite unexpectedly after the process of judgment in the underworld is mysteriously interrupted. There, Andrea performs the function of the ghost in Boccaccio, appearing before the audience on the stage as the ghost had appeared to the poet on his own 'stage' in the poet's chamber. This is a presence however which, unlike in Boccaccio, recreates as immediate background the marvellous journey into hell following Sackville:

> When I was slain my soul descended straight
> To pass the flowing stream of Acheron:
> But churlish Charon, only boatman there,
> Said that my rites of burial not perform'd,
> I might not sit amongst his passengers.
> Ere Sol had slept three nights in Thetis' lap
> And slak'd his smoking Chariot in her flood,
> By Don Horatio, our Knight Marshal's son,
> My funerals our obsequies were done.
> Then was the ferryman of hell content
> To pass me over to the slimy strond
> That leads to fell Avernus' ugly waves:
> There pleasing Cerebus with honey'd speech
> I pass'd the perils of the foremost porch.[5]

Once again, it is necessary to insist that Kyd's narrative, like Sackville's, functions as literal vision. Though the narrative itself may suggest something still far removed from a totally convincing projection of an embodied vision, it is certainly more than merely a fiction: there is no basis for allegorizing the narrative or reducing it to something else, for not taking it exactly as it appears as itself.

Moreover, the function of the Ghost and his narrative as vision would have been immeasurably enhanced when the transposition from one 'stage' to the other had been fully grasped. For the whole power of the Prologue depends on seeing it as a dramatic development of narrative procedure. What this meant was that the total vision which we see and hear on the stage, in the form of the Ghost and his narrative, was to be taken as the direct transposition of the vision acted out before the poet on his own stage when writing the play out in his chamber. The transposition implied an analogy between the audience watching and listening to the Ghost on stage and the poet watching and listening to it in his chamber; indeed, on the analogy of the poet in his chamber, the audience was being compelled to respond to what was taking place before it as a vision of their own, in a final extraordinary merging of the poet's vision with the vision of the audience. Something of this complex, metaphysical relation, one assumes, survives in the presentation of the Ghost in *Hamlet*, and it may explain the portentous intensity that unites us with the Ghost in his account.

One can see from developments in narrative tragedy that a perception of visionary development was intimately associated in this literature with the immediate inspiration of the chamber or the study, the concentrated solitude of which it is easy to imagine offering the poet just that marvellous setting for dynamic thinking in the complex metaphysical representation of his experience which he would well have been seeking. Nowhere is the sensitivity to the inspiration of this setting reflected in more dramatic terms than in that great inward realization in the drama of the Elizabethan Renaissance, *Dr. Faustus*. As Helen Gardner has noted 'the play begins and ends with

31

the hero in his study'.[6] Moreover, in a central scene from (one version of) that great play, the devious power of supersensible manifestation which Faustus brings with him to the court of the Emperor Claudius is explicitly projected by the Emperor as fulfilling that insistent identification with the sensible materialization of metaphorical thought brought into dynamic focus in the concentrated solitude of the study — that intimate, yearning *preoccupation* with supernatural vision — which one ought to look upon as a typical experience for the Renaissance:

Then, Doctor Faustus, mark what I shall say.
As I was sometime solitary set
Within my closet, sundry thoughts arose
About the honour of mine ancestors,
How they had won by prowess such exploits,
Got such riches, subdued so many kingdoms,
As we that do succeed, or they that shall
Hereafter possess our throne, shall,
I fear me, never attain to that degree
Of high renown and great authority;
Amongst which kings is Alexander the Great,
Chief spectacle of the world's pre-eminence,
The bright shining of whose glorious acts
Lightens the world with his reflecting beams,
As when I hear but motion made of him
It grieves my soul I never saw the man.
If, therefore, thou, by cunning of thine art,
Canst raise this man from hollow vaults below,
Where lies entomb'd this famous conqueror,
And bring with him his beauteous paramour,
Both in their right shapes, gesture and attire
They us'd to wear during their time of life,

Thou shalt both satisfy my just desire
And give me cause to praise thee whilst I live.[7]

In terms that are in keeping with this whole background material, the process of visionary engagement begins for Hamlet in a substantial sense, and to a degree greatly understressed in one aspect of the criticism of the play, in the experience of loss and division in the death of his splendidly noble father. One will acknowledge here as motive force initially the 'sorrowful imagination' of native narrative tradition with its embodiment of the experience of loss or death, or evil — or the tradition of the 'vision growing out of extreme sorrow' as Howard Baker accounts for it in his *Induction to Tragedy* — a tradition one can trace not only in the near-contemporary work of Sackville, as Baker does, but in as remote and individual a manifestation as one finds in Chaucer's 'Book of the Duchess'. In Hamlet's case, there is the added, complicating experience of subsequent disgrace and outrage:

HAM.: Thrift, thrift, Horatio! The funeral bak'd-meats
Did coldly furnish forth the marriage tables.
Would I had met my dearest foe in heaven
Or ever I had seen that day, Horatio!
My father — methinks I see my father.
HOR.: Where, my lord?
HAM.: In my mind's eye, Horatio!
HOR.: I saw him once; 'a was a goodly king.
HAM.: 'A was a man, take him for all in all,
I shall not look upon his like again.

(I.ii.180-188)[8]

Whether Hamlet's emotions are actually evolved enough in this part of the play to render the visionary figure of the Ghost fully believable as the projection of Hamlet's identification with his father in death is a moot point, one about which one can say at least that it is of no immediate concern to the play. It is sufficient for the play at this point that the relation is established within its own frank appropriation of the idea of the visionary possibility. Nor does this relation depend alone on the passage where Hamlet is shown claiming to 'see' his father 'in [his] mind's eye'. Powerful as such an evocation is already, it is rendered the more powerful when viewed as the surface expression of a crucial relation developed earlier when Hamlet is described 'seeking' with 'veiled lids' and 'eye' (I.ii.68-71) for his 'noble father in the dust'. One seeing is another. The play shows no embarrassment in associating the metaphorical import of Hamlet's mental 'seeing' as developed in the later passage with an even more literal relation in the earlier passage projecting vision as a miraculous extension of physical 'seeing'. Indeed, what is insistent about the initial action of this play is its status as a spectacular *fulfilment* of the rhetorical, wishing structure implicit in metaphorical vision:

HAM.:   *Would I* had met my dearest foe in heaven
          Or ever I had seen that day, Horatio!
          My father — *methinks I see* my father.
HOR.:   Where, my lord?
HAM.:   *In my mind's eye*, Horatio.

The rhetorical structure, through the implicit operation of the earlier (wilful) relation, now turns dramatically into literally true development, projecting indeed a faith in metaphysical possibility as extraordinary as anything in the age and characteristic of one aspect of it. This is the very development of literal fact that had escaped Richard II in his own quest for the visionary justification of an otherworldly power, greatly supporting and vindicating the common claim of these heroes to a knowledge of substantial reality in the experience of grief and outrage, in spite of the inevitable sceptical disbelief of their worlds. ('I have *that* within...'; '*there* lies the substance'). Moreover, Hamlet's engagement in vision gains further (although perhaps too obviously) in intensity from its association, when Hamlet speaks his mind to Horatio, with Horatio's experience of having once 'seen' Hamlet's father in life. It is a dramatic collocation of different orders of 'seeing' characteristic of this age's bold consideration of an accommodation of visionary realization at the level of the 'real' world. One is especially struck by the effort in this context to suggest that the Ghost possesses a vividness of reality directly comparable to bodily actuality. This is the gist of Horatio's response to the Ghost which he communicates at first to Marcellus and then to Hamlet:

HOR.:   Before my God, I might not this believe
       Without the sensible and true avouch
       Of mine own eyes.
MAR.:   Is it not like the King?

Hor.:   As thou art to thyself.

(I.i.56-59)

Hor.:   ...each word made true and good,
         The apparition comes. I knew your father;
         These hands are not more like.

(I.ii.210-212)

The difficulty which Hamlet faces in successfully grasping and retaining the complex substance of his experience at the interview is immediately conveyed to us after the disappearance of
the Ghost. We may choose, following a main
tradition, to attribute Hamlet's 'collapse' at this
point to his tragic shock and accompanying infir-
mity over the extremity of the corruption and evil
that has been revealed; for some, I believe
wrongly, it is a shock that, in fact, precedes the
revelation about the murder and that has thus
already significantly incapacitated Hamlet by the
time the murder is exposed. Such an emphasis on
the extremity of the evil known is no doubt true,
although it takes the rest of the play to make us
aware of what this evil finally involves. For the
emphasis *at this moment* points immediately for
cause to weakening in metaphysical intensity; as
Roy Walker has noted, it is immediately the problem of paling vision:

> Whether or not Hamlet will falter depends on his
> power to retain the stamp of this apocalyptic
> experience when the apparition is no longer be-
> fore him but visible only to the inward eye... the
> inward vision sinks below the level of conscious-
> ness.[9]

The breakdown of consciousness which accompanies the Ghost's disappearance constitutes for Hamlet a descent back into the ordinary world of sensible experience where the Ghost no longer provides a coherent and objective focus for the multi-leveled revelation of Hamlet's vision and where inward reality thus lacks the intense actuality and coherence of visionary *objectification*. The significance of this breakdown in *Hamlet* may be gleaned from parallel developments in *The Spanish Tragedy*. For the truly significant development in Kyd's Prologue was the final placing of the vision. The immediate vision of the Ghost, as in Boccaccio, remained 'real' enough, but the vision of hell had shifted here from being the immediate vision of the poet himself, as in Sackville, to being the remote vision of the Ghost. The literal function of narrative, of course, already ensured that even a vision presented at second-hand would be experienced by the audience as literal vision, even as immediate vision; but when it becomes clear that the Ghost has actually been narrating his vision from this side of the world, the vision undergoes an extraordinary deflation. What had been experienced by the audience at first as immediate vision becomes a vision suddenly placed in time and space beyond the world: indeed, in the bafflement which we re-enact with the Ghost in finding ourselves with him on this side of the world, it is as if the vision had never taken place, having vanished 'in the twinkling of an eye' (I.i.85), as quickly as the Ghost had been transported back to the world. Our initial experience of vision has convinced us that the vision has been real, but it is no longer immediate, and there is a sense in which it has even become unreal.

This ambiguity in the status of the vision is clinched when Kyd has the Ghost remark that in being transported from one place to the other, he has passed 'through the gates of horn' (I.i.82). G.K. Hunter has seen Andrea's return through the gates 'as dramatic equivalents to the introductory sequences of medieval dream allegory' ; from this, he concludes that 'the play may be viewed as what Andrea dreams'.[10] Yet this significance can hardly be obvious, for surely the use of the gates works the other way around: they confer the status of dream on Andrea's vision of the other-world, not on the world to which he returns which is the reality the dream-vision throws into relief.[11] That Andrea's dream is associated with the gates of horn suggests that Andrea's vision has been real, but once relegated to dream it becomes something less than itself — the memory of what has taken place on another plane. Nevertheless, we might add that Kyd's use of the dream-vision contrasts sharply in this respect with the mundane use made of it in the *Mirror*, as in Baldwin's dream of the Ghost of the Duke of York, which, though it puts the dream-vision into its traditional setting, presents something quite unlike the po-tently ambiguous reality of the dream-vision, since here the dream-vision amounts merely to 'fantasy' (1.59; p. 181).[12]

By contrast, in his Prologue Kyd relies, as we have seen, on a more subtle use of the vision-structure for the creation of 'real' perspective. First, the abstraction of the Ghost is given its own forceful 'reality' in the play through the theatrical transposition by which the poet's vision merges into the vision of the audience. The problem of abstraction posed by the descent into hell was likewise obviated through recourse to a literal appropriation of narrative: the Ghost's vision of the otherworld was to be experienced for itself; as elaborated, it drew on the sense of immediate wonder which one can easily imagine associated with the marvellous journey into hell. That Andrea's vision in the underworld should then suddenly undergo deflation is all the more extraordinary considering the pains Kyd has taken in the Prologue for the creation of perspective. But the deflation would seem to be crucial to Kyd's theme. The same breakdown in reality, with its new, paradoxical awareness of limitation-*in*-reality, could be demonstrated in the progression of Hieronimo's speeches, making Kyd the first amongst Elizabethan dramatists to embody, to his own limited degree of realization, a new expression of the fortunes and significance of sorrowful imagination:

HIER.: And art thou come, Horatio, from the depth,
To ask for justice..
....
But let me look on my Horatio:
SENEX: Ah my good lord, I am not your young son.
HIER.: What, not my son? Thou, then, a fury art,

39

> Sent from the empty kingdom of black night
> To summon me to make appearance
> Before grim Minos and just Rhadamanth,
> To plague Hieronimo that is remiss
> And seeks not vengeance for Horatio's death.
> SENEX: I am a grieved man, and not a ghost,
> That came for justice for my murder'd son.
> HIER.: Ay, now I know thee, now thou nam'st thy son,
> Thou art the lively image of my grief:.................
> ....
> And all this sorrow riseth for thy son:
> And selfsame sorrow feel I for my son.

(III.xiii.133ff.)

And so we may imagine Hamlet saying: 'And selfsame sorrow feel I for my father'. Thus, just when the self might have counted on its old capacity to crystallize the visionary power of an otherworldly realization, it finds itself suddenly tragically isolated, conscious of itself as possessed of an identity known in direct relation to its separation from such capacity. It would take an exposition far beyond the limited scope of this essay to elaborate the full significance of the dramatic breakdown in imaginative capacity to which the hero is now subjected. Yet, already one can appreciate the picturesque pathos and gravity of the change now coming over the scene as the hero is suddenly jolted *out* of his full identity with an otherworldly reality and world basis. Gone suddenly is the initial certitude of an original connexion immediately linking the hero in his sorrow to its visionary realization in the otherworld. In its stead is now the *isolated* human sorrow, more real certainly in 'our' sense of what is real, but emerging, as one can see, as the sorrowful separation into a consciousness of self whose identity is thus defined through the fact that it is known in direct relation to this tragedy of lost contact with an otherworldly reality and world-basis; a contact and capacity from which the human 'self' is distinguished by its separateness but from which it cannot originally be separately conceived; for the emergence of the human self represents in this manifestation pre-eminently a lament over the loss of such capacity.

Hamlet, it is true, breaks through to another, final 'vision' of the Ghost. And what is emphasized to us by this difficult, extraordinary reunion of mother, son and father in states so hopelessly and irreversibly changed from the innocent condition in which they had known each other before the murder, is the tremendous pity of the family break-up and separation. The pity of that predicament is emphasized to us the more as a result of Hamlet's effort, as a consequence of this separation, to substantiate what must seem to Hamlet and to us the only available means left for these three to *justify* themselves again. That effort is to be seen when Hamlet desperately seeks to direct Gertrude's attention to the reality of his vision of his father's Ghost and what this portends of *hope*:

QUEEN: Whereon do you look?
HAMLET: On him, on him! *Look* you how pale he glares.
His form and cause conjoin'd preaching to stones,

41

Would make them capable. *Do not look upon me,—*
Lest with this piteous action you convert
My stern effects; then what I have to do
Will want true colour — tears perchance for blood.

QUEEN: To whom do you speak this?

HAMLET: Do you see nothing there?

QUEEN: Nothing at all; yet all that is I see.

HAMLET: Nor did you nothing hear?

Queen: No, nothing but ourselves.

Hamlet: Why, *look* you there. *Look how* it steals away.
My father, in his habit as he liv'd!
Look where he goes even now out at the portal.

(III.iv.124-136)

Hamlet's directing action with Gertrude is his latest and most poignant attempt to bridge that impenetrable gap between the *reality* of vision, on the one hand, and, on the other, the desperate insistence of a speech entirely given over to the possibility of visionary realization in its metaphysical reaches and at its metaphysical limits. But with this last experience of the ultimate elusiveness of the Ghost and his reality, an old possibility of realization passes away for good, having, with its disappearance, ushered in a new significance for sorrow.

We have seen, then, how *Hamlet*, and its predecessor *The Spanish Tragedy*, build on the entirely extraordinary faith of that age in a power of 'sorrowful imagination' as literally true development. Only a careful consideration of the complex developments from narrative to dramatic tragedy will allow us to appreciate clearly the extraordinary daring and depth of originality entailed in reviving a faith of that kind. Sackville, in breaking away from the highly conventionalized mode of the *Mirror*, was the first to restore vital power to an ancient and venerable visionary tradition. By the time *Hamlet* was being written, awareness of the possibilities of sorrowful imagination had become general, as is evidenced by the Emperor's speech from the 1604 A-text of *Dr. Faustus*. But in further adapting that tradition to the tragic self-consciousness of his own time, Kyd must be credited with having displayed quite as much daring as had Sackville, breaking with tradition while yet preserving a wonderfully comprehensive sense of continuity with the past. *Hamlet* brings both the tradition and the new tragic self-consciousness into a further relation of consummate power and poignancy. And in an age as sceptical as our own, when the question of our relation to the possibility of an otherworldly experience has all but ceased to possess any direct urgency for so many of us, one can only marvel at the profoundly searching spirit that could make a traditional power of otherworldly realization once again available to the Elizabethan imagination, as well as at the acute understanding which that imagination reveals of one, peculiar dimension of the modern sorrowful self. That dimension both Shakespeare and Kyd would seem, as a consequence of their traditional power, to have been in an especially privileged position to see in terms of an otherworldly relation.

II

Sexuality

A consistently progressive view of Hamlet's overwhelming engagement in visionary destiny has been greatly undermined in the criticism of this play by a prominent opinion which has stressed Hamlet's revulsion at his mother's sexuality as the *exclusive*, fundamental motivation in Hamlet's experience. Such an opinion rests strongly, though not entirely, on a reading of Hamlet's emotions about his mother's marriage in his first soliloquy which has been taken to express Hamlet's melancholic disgust, emotions before whose intensity the revelation of the murder and the sense of horror it inspires have been felt to be secondary and superfluous. As a matter of fact, what is more properly described as Hamlet's outraged despair over his mother's marriage constitutes at the point of Hamlet's first soliloquy an entirely *new* emphasis in Hamlet's grief, for until then Hamlet's melancholic outburst is one which we are bound to refer on the whole to Hamlet's grief over the loss of his father, and to the sorry state of affairs to which the 'world' has come since the death of his father. Hamlet begins his account of his feelings in his soliloquy with precisely this emphasis:

> That it should come to this!
> But two months dead! Nay, not so much, not two.
> So excellent a king that was to this
> Hyperion to a satyr; so loving to my mother,
> That he might not beteem the winds of heaven
> Visit her face too roughly. Heaven and earth!
> Must I remember? Why, she would hang on him

As if increase of appetite had grown
By what it fed on; and yet, within a month —
Let me not think on't. Frailty, thy name is woman! —
A little month, or ere those shoes were old
With which she followed my poor father's body,
Like Niobe, all tears — why she, even she —
O God! a beast that wants discourse of reason
Would have mourn'd longer — married with my
    uncle,
My father's brother; but no more like my father
Than I to Hercules.

(I.ii.137-153)

I see no evidence in Hamlet's soliloquy of an *active* disgust for his mother's sexuality, but rather profound outraged despair stemming, on the contrary, from active pride in the sexual splendour of his father, which is specifically what has made marriage to Claudius insupportable, the marriage being an unbelievable display of womanly weakness and insensitivity. Thus, when it is revealed that what occupies Hamlet specifically is his mother's hastiness in marrying a second time, the revelation is one that is already deeply conditioned by our sense of the outrage it represents to the memory of Hamlet's father who projected in Hamlet's eyes a contrastingly noble condition. 'Let me not think on't': think on what? On Gertrude's marriage with Claudius. Yet the direction of the thought is predetermined by the earlier 'Must I remember?', where it is clear that Hamlet is *also* thinking on the splendid union between Gertrude and Hamlet's father now so pitifully outraged.

Nor is Hamlet's identification with his father in grief, subtle and profound as it is here in expression, restricted to these terms, for there is the further suggestion that the motive force in Hamlet's experience lies in his ultimate identification with his father in death and God's reality, including the implicit, favourable judgment assumed to have been bestowed on Hamlet's father, in contrast to the present ignoble life of his mother with Claudius:

O, that this too too solid flesh would melt,
Thaw, and resolve itself into a dew!
Or that the Everlasting had not fix'd
His canon 'gainst self-slaughter! *O God! God!*
How weary, stale, flat, and unprofitable,
Seem to me all the uses of this world!
Fie on't! Ah, fie! 'tis an unweeded garden,
That grows to seed; things rank and gross in nature
Possess it merely. That it should come to this!
But two months dead! Nay, not so much, not two.
So excellent a king that was to this
Hyperion to a satyr; so loving to my mother,
That he might not beteem the winds of heaven
Visit her face too roughly. Heaven and earth!
Must I remember? Why, she would hang on him
As if increase of appetite had grown
By what it fed on; and yet, within a month —
....
                        why she, even she —
O God!..
.... married with my uncle...

(I.ii.129ff)

And so, when Horatio finally breaks the wondrous news of his father's visitation, the terms in which Hamlet expresses his impatience with Horatio to tell on are all in keeping with this fundamental motivating inspiration:

For God's love, let me hear.

(I.ii.195)

With the Ghost's account, however, comes a dramatic re-orientation in Hamlet's view. For from the moment the Ghost begins to reveal himself at the interview, it is established for a start that judgment on Hamlet's father has *not* been favourable as Hamlet has supposed, thus greatly complicating and intensifying the grieved pity Hamlet already feels over the loss of his father in death:

Thus was I, sleeping, by a brother's hand
Of life, of crown, of queen, at once dispatch'd;
Cut off even in the blossoms of my sin,
Unhous'led, disappointed, unanel'd;
No reck'ning made, but sent to my account
With all my imperfections on my head.
O, horrible! O, horrible! most horrible!
If thou hast nature in thee, bear it not....

(I.v.74-81)

At the heart of the outrage to Hamlet's father is the suggestion of a horrible inhumanity represented by a murder whose significance for Hamlet's father is that he was 'Cut off in the blossoms of his sin'. It is a strange phrase, because of the violent juxtaposition we get of 'sin' with all the positive qualities invoked for us by the term 'blossoms'. Yet a somewhat complex adjustment on our part *will* allow us to penetrate the paradoxical and indeed quite terrible significance of the phrase. In our post-Romantic age, we will be inclined to overlook that 'nature' almost always automatically involved for the Elizabethans the *sexual* correlative; when we consider, furthermore, the overwhelming and contradicting influence of Calvin and of Luther at this time, we shall then be in a position to see in Shakespeare's use of the phrase the recognition of a power of judgment bearing down on the sexual optimism of the Elizabethans. What the phrase appears meant to convey, to the tragic confounding of Hamlet's aesthetic sense, is a judgment on the sinfulness of even the richest and noblest sexuality, what had formerly been assumed, that is, to be the expression of a noble beauty in nature fully embodied for Hamlet in the sexual splendour of his father as a man, but which metaphysical events have now revealed to be finally punishable in the otherworld.

The objection will perhaps be raised that the Ghost at this very interview speaks of his 'love' as being 'of that dignity/That it went hand in hand even with the vow/I made to her in marriage' which would seem to suggest a 'love' that was sound. In fact, the Ghost is here referring to his faithfulness; faithfulness on his part does not imply soundness in the relationship; and we learn here there was Gertrude's adultery with Claudius, and that already implies a relationship between Gertrude and the elder Hamlet no longer sound. But in any case, for Calvin, as for Luther, neither faithfulness nor marriage could *ever* ensure soundness in the sexual relationship; or as Luther puts it:

...nothing can cure libido, not even marriage...[1]

And the Ghost's sudden revelation captures all that is most disturbing in the Protestant view, namely that such a significance for sexual love could not be known for certain except as a judgment in the otherworld. Such a reading of the Ghost's situation will explain what has long baffled critics, as to why Hamlet should treat the sexual problem as if it were a universal affliction. For the effect of this revelation on Hamlet, we must assume, must be to make of his father's fate a universal embodiment of the tragedy of sexuality.

The motivating force behind Gertrude's adultery and the murder it engenders is an inhumanity of the profoundest implication. It isn't merely that a bestial lust leads to (or is involved in) the inhumanity of murder; ultimately, the significance of such lust is to emphasize the lust in all love, involving a murder that is *itself* a violent arraignment of sexual love, leading to judgment in the otherworld for Hamlet's father. In this arraignment we find represented that darker Lutheran view which is now brought into further tension with another view that is yet reserved, more indulgent and typically Elizabethan, according to which sexual love is innocent, and a normal indulgence of nature to be atoned for and settled (in preparation for the otherworld) through the customary religious rites:

> Cut off even in the blossoms of my sin
> Unhous'led, disappointed, unanel'd;
> No reck'ning made, but sent to my account
> With all my imperfections on my head.
> O, horrible! O, horrible! most horrible!

It is to full implications of these most complex developments, in themselves extremely unwieldy, and not, as has been suggested, to some mysterious psychotic disturbance, that we are to ascribe Hamlet's later hysterical preoccupation with sexuality. It is how Hamlet's original sense of the moral-emotional outrage against his father is ultimately experienced. Such hysteria is not to be confused with the 'hysteria' over his mother's sexuality displayed in the first soliloquy which has been much exaggerated and, I believe, in any case, misinterpreted. The 'hysteria' expressed there measures the gap between his mother's lust for Claudius and the innocent intensity of her sexual love for Hamlet's father. This distinction is not merely intensified, it is tragically confounded by later revelations about the sexual implications of his father's murder, and no doubt the outrage is the greater for this. To this is added the horror of punishment in the otherworld, all of which calls for full and immediate revenge. Thus, in his preoccupation with sexuality, Hamlet is not giving vent to a disturbance independent of the play's pattern of crime and punishment, with implications strictly for Hamlet's character or his view of life.[2] On the contrary, he is coming to grips with the disturbance at the very heart of the play: with the horror of a sexual judgment which leads directly to punishment in the otherworld for Hamlet's father.

And so we get that tortuously pained and tragic accusation, so complex, which Hamlet brings against Gertrude in the closet scene.

> Such an act
> That blurs the grace and blush of modesty;
> Calls virtue hypocrite; takes off the rose
> From the fair forehead of an innocent love,
> And sets a blister there; makes marriage-vows
> As false as dicers' oaths. O, such a deed
> As from the body of contraction plucks
> The very soul, and sweet religion makes
> A rhapsody of words. Heaven's face does glow
> O'er this solidity and compound mass
> With heated visage, as against the doom —
> Is thought-sick at the act.

(III.iv.40-51)

One of the more significant features of Hamlet's complex accusation here is that it begins with an account of blighted love which would seem from the context to apply to the relationship between Hamlet's mother and father but which might equally apply to the relationship between Hamlet and Ophelia (it is not, as E.M.W. Tillyard claimed[3], merely a reference to the latter). The ambiguity is significant and a clue to Hamlet's behaviour towards Ophelia in the nunnery-scene. Hamlet's behaviour here is not to be explained as a mysterious, fundamental disturbance regarding sexuality, one essentially *unrelated* to the murder; on the contrary, it is precisely Hamlet's disposition in the scene to view the nature of this relationship strictly in relation to the sexual implications of the murder, particularly its implications for the innocence of love. Thus, when Hamlet characterizes consummated love as something that would make of Ophelia a 'breeder of sinners' (by this, of course, Hamlet has specifically in mind a consummated love with him), Hamlet is acting on the assumption that all love is lust, when seen from the perspective of otherworldly judgment, as true of Hamlet and Ophelia as it was of his father and mother. The effect of this perspective on Hamlet is to persuade him that although he is himself 'indifferent honest' (III.i.122) and likely in the figure of Ophelia to be 'inoculated' by 'virtue' (117), he is inevitably bound to 'relish of it' (118).

Yet such an explanation as I have given could not *alone* account for Hamlet's peculiar hysteria, either in the nunnery-scene or the closet-scene, which seems finally to emerge from the murder's full paradoxical implications for love. These set in tragic conflict alongside the otherworldly knowledge of love as lust a lingering sense of the fundamental innocence of love. Hamlet's behaviour in the nunnery-scene is ultimately explained by the knowledge that he could not from an otherworldly perspective have loved Ophelia with the innocence he supposed; yet, the

55

knowledge itself is endowed with the full pain of a tragic discovery conflicting with the more immediate knowledge that he did and still does. And it is thus that we are given a sense of what has been lost, and must be abandoned: belief in a love which ennobles nature characterized in the play by the love between Hamlet and Ophelia and that originally assumed of Hamlet's father and mother, what the play elaborates as the 'rose' in love (III.iv.42-43) embodying 'rose of May' (IV.v.154) — contrasting with 'A took my father.../ With all his crimes broad blown, as flush as May' (III.iii.80-81) — that itself held the 'expectancy and rose of the fair state' (III.i.152), but which tragic events have revealed to be merely the 'primrose path' (I.iii.50) — consider 'the blossoms of my sin' (I.v.76) — to 'sulphurous and tormenting flames' (I.v.3).

Hamlet's behaviour towards Ophelia is thus finally bred of (and fully explained by) Hamlet's new tragic sense of the sexual paradox. In this tragic condition, it is evident that there can no longer be much significance for the kind of compromise honesty once treated as an absolute honesty, till the Ghost's revelation exposed it as compromise, which once settled the paradox by properly subordinating sexual nature to the rites of religion, specifically to marriage. It is with this consideration in mind, then, that we must approach Hamlet's new sense of the power of sexuality:

...for the power of beauty will sooner transform
honesty from what it is to a bawd than the force
of honesty can translate beauty into his likeness.
This was sometime a paradox, but now the time
gives it proof.

(III.i.111-115)

Here, in Hamlet's reference to 'honesty' the
more obscure sense of 'genuineness' or 'legiti-
macy' has been grafted onto the more obvious,
immediate sense of 'chastity' though a statement
viewing the conflict between sexuality and chastity implicitly in relation to the conflict between
sexuality and marriage as brought out by the
murder. By the latter conflict I mean primarily the
limitations of marriage as a means of restraining
and sanctifying the sexual drive, limitations exposed by the revelations about his fate made by
Hamlet's father, but also and more obviously the
sexual considerations which led Hamlet's mother
to violate her marriage to Hamlet's father thus
ultimately bringing about (whether the subsequent marriage to Claudius was a direct cause of
the murder or not) Hamlet's full tragic discovery
about marriage. Given this last connexion, it
seems inevitable that Hamlet should come to see
Gertrude's marriage to Claudius as a living embodiment of all that marriage has been shown not
to be; likewise inevitable that the question of an
honest love with Ophelia, which could only be
kept honest by marriage, should drive Hamlet to
say with special reference to the implications of
Gertrude's marriage: 'I say we will have no moe

marriage' (III.i.147).

The tragic situation underlying this climactic utterance is brought to full statement in the passage from the closet-scene already quoted. We may summarize that situation by tracing the argument implied. The suggestion is that the 'union' (and marriage) between Gertrude and Claudius (and the murder it involves) has implied a blighted love, not only between Gertrude and the elder Hamlet but also between Hamlet and Ophelia. This is so in the sense that the union involves the *falsification* of marriage. Apart from the fact that it represents the violation of one marriage by another, the full effect of the union has been to destroy the illusion that marriage necessarily sanctifies love, for what has been exposed, *sub species aeternitatis*, are the limitations of marriage alone before the power of sexuality. What has been finally lost, in fact, is an innocent perspective on religion as a whole, what had formerly made it possible to indulge the sweetness of sexual love and at the same time (and without contradiction) submit to the judgments and practices of religion: that 'sweet religion' which tragic events have revealed to be merely a 'rhapsody of words'.

In the rest of the speech, Hamlet goes on to claim through some typical Shakespearean hyperbole, that the sexual outrage has been so monstrous and so appalling to Heaven, what it threatens is the break-up of the world itself, and the immediate precipitation of doom and judgment. This is more than mere hyperbole. In being represented as 'thought-sick', Heaven embodies Hamlet himself, the suggestion being that in his psychological experience of the outrage Hamlet has to a degree literally united himself with Heaven in the sense that he has come to possess as a result of his experience intimations of a visionary eruption in the world. The propelling force behind the anticipated eruption lies in Hamlet's profound experience of outrage. From the representation of Heaven's face this is emphasized as a prodigious sense of shame, but a sense of shame represented significantly as the lust which has compelled it, as 'heated visage' suggests simultaneously the blush of modesty and sexual ardor. The ambiguity in the representation of Heaven's face would seem to be used by Shakespeare, finally, to build up the image of Heaven, on the verge of Judgment, blushing over itself as a Great Whore. Whatever we may think of this as an intimation of the projected scope of judgment in this play, it seems clear that Shakespeare meant by it to project some sense of the ultimate implications of Hamlet's psychological experience, here specifically as it relates to his awareness of lust as a universal condition portending judgment for all in otherworldly terms.

To Gertrude's further exasperated appeal challenging an account of the complex accusation Hamlet brings against her — 'Ay me, what act,/ That roars so loud and thunders in the index?' (III.iv.51-52) — Hamlet replies, typically, not with any direct reply, but, as if as counteraction to Gertrude's contemptuous disbelief over his abstraction, by penetrating again to the very contrast between his father and Claudius the wilful realization of which in himself accounts for the process that leads initially to the crystallization of the Ghost:

Look here upon this picture and on this...

(III.iv.53ff)

One may look upon Hamlet's return to the contrast between his father and Claudius at this point of the play merely as a regressive emphasis. To my understanding, it occasions in Hamlet rather some of the most intense, thinking penetration of that power of lust defying all reason which, whatever the precise causality in time, was not only the animating cause in the murder of Hamlet's father but the appalling occasion of Hamlet's revelation about a supernatural judgment testifying even more conclusively to that power's horror. When one bears in mind this further supernatural extension of the tragedy it becomes clear that the terms of Hamlet's penetration of the matter at this point are entirely essential, if pitifully inadequate and baffled:

What devil was't
That thus hath cozen'd you at hoodman-blind?

(III.iv.76-77)

The outright hysteria that eventually emerges in Hamlet's baffled account only yields more point and penetration to Hamlet's further effort from here to reach out (as with a searchlight) to the basis of a controlling and corrective good lying amidst such power of lust, which Hamlet desperately assumes must be there in the being *in reality*, to be touched off, if good is to prevail:

> Eyes without feeling, feeling without sight,
> Ears without hands or eyes, smelling sans all,
> Or but a sickly part of one true sense
> Could not so mope. *O shame! where is thy blush?*
>
> (III.iv.78-81)

The power of the address to hell which follows comes thus from the literal object of Hamlet's thinking at this point:

> Rebellious hell,
> If thou can'st mutine in a matron's bones,
> To flaming youth let virtue be as wax
> And melt in her own fire...
>
> (III.iv.82-85)

and at its climax gives ironic sign of the same desperate nihilism, the same utter lack of positive confidence about reality, if in a less advanced form, as will animate the later projections of Lear:

> ...proclaim no shame
> When the compulsive ardour gives the charge,
> Since frost itself as actively doth burn...

finally invoking the ultimate horrible transformation and inversion:

> And reason panders will.
>
> (III.iv.85-88)

III

Revenge

Emphasis on the questionableness to Hamlet of Ghost and revenge stems inevitably from an emphasis on a sceptical consciousness implicit in the play. The latter is an emphasis which has been developed, in this century, in several forms,[1] each with its own distinctive moral-metaphysical perspective on the action and, in each, central reference is made to 'all those speculations about death and what comes after death'[2] which, in addition to the Ghost's ambiguous demands, would appear to have marked the play out un-mistakeably as a tragedy of doubt and uncertainty. In this extended and highly flexible form, the sceptical viewpoint constitutes one of the major approaches to *Hamlet* in this century. It is, in its main features, demonstrably a modern development of the nineteenth-century emphasis on the play as a tragedy of thought and irresolution,[3] and, thus, the modern version of two major manifestations of the projection of Hamlet as the 'myth character of the doubting, self-contemplating intellectual'.[4] Since the larger critical tradition which I have just outlined is one on which a good deal of attention has already been lavished, it would be supererogatory of me to attempt to represent it. My concern, rather, is with one, peripheral manifestation of this tradition as it bears on the authenticity and integrity of the Ghost. The Ghost's appearance and comportment, we are told, are such as to warrant intense doubt and self-questioning on Hamlet's part. On closer examination, this issue turns out to be one which many critics have felt to be subsumed in the natural impression received from the play that the Ghost is genuinely the spirit of Hamlet's dead father.[5] Perplexing doubts, it is true, remain, for it is undeniable that both Horatio and Hamlet, when addressing themselves to the Ghost, act on the knowledge that the Ghost might possibly not be genuine. But in the structure of the exposition, such doubts are merely the measure of the Ghost's overwhelming power of engagement. For it is a fact of exposition that all doubts are ultimately subsumed in the larger emphasis on the wonder of the Ghost's *reality*, his pitiful majestic distress, and on his significance as an embodiment of a visionary revelation the determination of which must be extorted from him at all costs.[6]

The authenticity of the Ghost, however, has also been questioned on the grounds that in the nature of its demands, there exists a fundamental contradiction and an absence of integrity, an objection which centres around the command to revenge. This has been deemed questionable on the grounds that revenge is an unnatural and strictly barbarous principle inconsistent with and repugnant to the civilized-Christian viewpoint of the play. This is a reading which has had an extremely wide acceptance.[7] But implied in most criticisms of revenge as an unnatural and barbaric command is the idea of revenge as a physical act and punishment only, even though it is a crucial fact and one which could not, one feels, fail to be remarked, that revenge is enjoined not as a physical punishment primarily but as a metaphysical one designed to express Hamlet's complex relation to his father's murder and to pass divine judgment and, in this sense, enjoined as a sacred, heroic and creative act.[8] It is simply untrue and grossly unfair to the passionate majesty and visionary awesomeness[9] of the interview between Hamlet and the Ghost to say that the call for revenge is 'lugubrious'[10] or anything less than consummately engaging and extraordinary. It is precisely these aspects of the scene which lift the Ghost's demands onto a higher metaphysical level of engagement the moral unity of which we are not meant to doubt, remote and archaic as it may all appear to us to be today.

Nevertheless, this is not to deny questioning in the play at a more evolved stage, sometime after Hamlet's impression of the interview with the Ghost has faded, which I should like to bring forward by focusing first on a significant ambiguity in the following passage:

> I am myself indifferent honest, but yet I could accuse me of such things that it were better my mother had not borne me: I am very proud, revengeful, ambitious; with more *offences* at my beck than I have thoughts to put them in, imagination to give them shape, or time to act them in.

(III.i.122-127)

It is obvious that the passage, in context, is meant to be taken partly as self-dramatization craftily designed by Hamlet to reinforce (whether or not Hamlet assumes Polonius and the King to be immediately present) the erratic judgment of Hamlet's behaviour associated through Rosencrantz and Guildenstern with the King. The dramatization, however, is not entirely convincing, at least not to the King, who comes away as alarmed as ever, unconvinced that what obsesses Hamlet is either love or ambition. If this is so, it is partly because as with so much else in this scene, as with Hamlet's dealings with the Court generally, the passage constitutes, at the same time as it is meant to be evasively self-dramatizing, an alarmingly genuine if a typically enigmatic revelation about Hamlet's state of mind. To the King, on one level, it represents (and is meant to represent) a monstrous threat on his life judged to be of general 'danger' to him (III.i.167); to Hamlet (and to us) it is a suggestion of the projected 'revenge', on this level strangely exaggerated in part from genuine bafflement *now* about its import. The effect on Hamlet of his bafflement strangely is to suggest that *it is he himself who is monstrous.* The reason for this is provided through a highly significant ambiguity in Hamlet's use of 'offences' (III.i.12). This can be taken to mean either the 'offences' Hamlet threatens to inflict on Claudius or the 'offences' already inflicted by Claudius on Hamlet. Thus, a first suggestion is that one set of 'offences' is simultaneously the other; a second suggestion (drawn from what follows) is that both 'offences' are outside Hamlet's power of control and monstrous to Hamlet because of this. And so it is because

Claudius 'offences' cannot be properly controlled for purposes of revenge that Claudius' 'offences' become Hamlet's 'offences' in an *identical* sense, the latter representing in fact *the literal repetition of the former*.

The profound suggestion of literal identity emerges from yet another passage taking us back to Hamlet's disturbing projection of himself as Pyrrhus in the Player's speech about the slaughter of Priam, a passage unconsciously 'called for' by Hamlet. I am referring here to the section in the speech which depicts Pyrrhus in 'unequal' combat with Priam, particularly the point of hesitation as Pyrrhus is just about to descend on Priam:

> his [Priam's] antique sword,
> Rebellious to his arm, lies where it falls,
> Repugnant to command. Unequal match'd,
> Pyrrhus at Priam drives, in rage strikes wide;
> But with the whiff and wind of his fell sword
> Th' unnerved father falls. Then senseless Ilium,
> Seeming to feel this blow, with flaming top
> Stoops to his base, and with a hideous crash
> Takes prisoner Pyrrhus' ear. For, lo! his sword,
> Which was declining on the milky head
> Of reverend Priam, seem'd i' th' air to stick.
> So, as a painted tyrant, Pyrrhus stood
> And, like a neutral to his will and matter,
> Did nothing.

(II.ii.463-476)

Once again there is a highly significant am-biguity, in the representation of Pyrrhus. It is obvious that as a 'painted tyrant' suspended over the helpless Priam, Pyrrhus is designed to suggest, in Kenneth Muir's words,[11] 'the ruthless king-killer Claudius'; less obvious is the fact that, hesitating in this fashion, 'like a neutral to his will and matter', Pyrrhus simultaneously suggests Hamlet. I believe Muir is wrong in claiming that insofar as it concerns Hamlet, the suggestion is that Pyrrhus is the 'ruthless avenger Hamlet wished to be himself'. In fact, the representation of hesitation and stagnancy so suggestive of Hamlet seems to point rather to the opposite conclusion: that Pyrrhus is precisely the 'ruthless avenger' Hamlet does not wish to be. The connexion between revenge and murder, moreover, is more than a matter of common ruthlessness. If Pyrrhus' deed suggests both murder and revenge at once, as Pyrrhus suggests at once both Claudius and Hamlet, then up to a point revenge *is* murder, as Hamlet is Claudius; revenge is in some sense the *direct* expression of murder. This is so, I believe, in the sense that the energy and violence of Claudius' crime are *literally* the energy and violence of Hamlet's projected revenge — the two exist up to a point as *one* in Hamlet's mind, as Hamlet's psychological experience of the crime. However, if revenge and murder are one in the sense and to the extent I suggest, then the risk is that revenge will not emerge as itself, as an action taken to redress the violence of murder and, therefore, as an action morally different from murder, but as a literal *repetition* of the murder. Hence Hamlet's 'doubt', hence the hesitation.

By another ambiguity in the representation of Pyrrhus (one ultimately conveying profound pathos) Hamlet's 'scruple' in revenge is linked directly to the 'scruple' which in murder Claudius ought to have had but didn't, or the 'scruple' which he did have but chose to ignore. It is the scruple of conscience which could have averted the evil in the first place and, thus, spared Hamlet the anxiety of his own, the 'scruple-in-murder' which for a moment substitutes for the 'scruple-in-revenge' as the *other* countercheck to evil whose failure at the time is especially to be regretted now that it has made the operations of conscience in countering evil tragically complicated for Hamlet. And it is out of a sense of the complications inherent in this that for a moment the play harks back pathetically to the thought of what Hamlet might have been spared had Claudius submitted to his 'scruple' when the moral conflict was clearer and easier, before the complications of murder rendered the operations of conscience tragically problematic.

The point of the ambiguity is not to imply that Hamlet ought to act on his scruple as Claudius ought to have acted on his, anymore than the play assumes that revenge is, from a moral judgment, *necessarily* like murder. The play's meditation at this point stems rather from the fact that the evil set loose by murder, which conscience alone could not avert, makes the revenge required to restrain it tragically complicated, posing the problem of a violent action to be done in 'perfect conscience' (V.ii.67), perfect integrity of being, and so raising the spectre of whether the act of revenge is ' to be or not to be'. Thus, when Hamlet, having just narrated the details of the sea-adventure to Horatio, later rationalizes the need for revenge by invoking the fullness of the evidence of Claudius' evil as well as the implicit evidence of a proliferating evil:

> Is't not perfect conscience
> To quit him with this arm?

(V.ii.67-68)

he is (perhaps wilfully) obscuring for a moment the tragic complications inherent in countering evil with revenge. When he goes on to ask of himself if it is not:

> to be damn'd
> To let this canker of our nature come
> In further evil?

(V.ii.68-70)

he suggests through this by a significant *inversion* of the implications of revenge which suggest that Hamlet's revenge is bound up with Claudius' damnation, that it is as much to be damned himself to let Claudius' evil rage unchecked as it is also to be damned, in a sense for the moment obscured by Hamlet, to counter evil with an improper revenge.

Thus, in Levin's phrase[12], the problem is how to know what to do, but not in Levin's sense — that the rational limits of human knowledge make it impossible for us or for Hamlet to understand the exact significance and purpose of the Ghost or if Hamlet is to accomplish his revenge. Here the powers of human knowledge are adequate enough. It is rather that the normal, rational limits of human knowledge are inadequate to compel the tragic complexity of Hamlet's experience into the moral unity required for Hamlet to fulfil his purposes which demand the phenomenally integrating power of an original visionary knowledge that would seem to be irrecoverable. Thus, to the extent that the required revenge is unknown to Hamlet (in the visionary sense) and merely known (in the rational sense) it is tragically problematic, in the sense that there is a double danger of mistaking the known for the unknown and deferring to the lack of knowledge at the expense of the known, corresponding to the double fact that it is to be damned both to execute an improper revenge and not to execute a revenge at all. As such, both dangers measure what is right and what is possible: on the one hand, an *ideal* revenge representing a proportionate violence done in 'perfect conscience'; on the other, an *immediate* revenge to be measured according to its 'distance' from the other.

Both considerations are crucial in helping us judge the complex effect of the prayer-scene, which seems to be precisely about the multiple ironies and complications connected with Hamlet's attempt to conceive of the required 'horridness' in revenge.

The conflicting judgments which have been brought to bear on Hamlet's behaviour in the prayer-scene make this, in Levin's phrase[13], the *vexata questio* of critical interpretation (second perhaps only to the ending of *King Lear*, and whether *Lear* is finally a pessimistic or optimistic play). It is a striking indication of the conflicting responses elicited by this scene that the 'reasons' given for Hamlet's delay have been traced to considerations of humaneness on the one hand, and hubris and monstrous inhumanity on the other. Thus, Helen Gardner (echoing G. Wilson Knight) has argued that the scene appeals to our sense that we do not wish 'to see Hamlet stab a defenceless kneeling man'[14]. Similarly, Peter Alexander (echoing Bradley) has brought attention to standards of humane conduct which keep Hamlet from 'stabbing a villain in the back'[15]. The purpose (and effect) of the scene, according to this position, is to create a set of conditions which, by appealing to considerations of humaneness, make revenge seem immediately inappropriate and ironic.

It is a glaring flaw in Alexander's argument, however, that he does not address himself to the apparent monstrousness of the 'reasons' Hamlet actually gives. These cannot be explained merely by reference to the complementary virtue of 'toughness' in that general disposition of character in Hamlet whose heroic distinction for Alexander consists in being 'humane without loss of toughness'. The effect of Alexander's argument, in fact,

74

is to suggest that the reasons given for Hamlet's delay (which Alexander draws, like Gardner, from the audience's sense of what is right and appropriate in the circumstances) are the explicit reasons Hamlet gives, another oversight which makes Alexander's interpretation of this scene finally unsatisfactory. Helen Gardner is herself more carefully explicit. She glosses the 'depth of hatred' to be found in the reasons Hamlet gives as an 'outlet' for 'baffled rage':

> No.
> Up, sword, and know thou a more horrid hent.
> When he is drunk asleep, or in his rage;
> Or in th' incestuous pleasure of his bed;
> At game, a-swearing, or about some act
> That has no relish of salvation in't —
> Then trip him, that his heels may kick at heaven,
> And that his soul may be as damn'd and black
> As hell, whereto it goes.

(III.iii.87-95)

On the other hand, for those for whom Hamlet's reasons given here are neither an expression of bafflement, nor insincere[16], in whom the inclination (following Waldock) is to assume that Hamlet 'means what he says'[17], the purpose of the scene is to draw attention to Hamlet's hubris, to show how in 'reaching out too far in his calculations'[18], Hamlet misses the 'perfect moment'[19] for revenge. Here emphasis has been given to Hamlet 'playing at God'[20]: 'the mere death of Claudius is not enough... he will have him eternally damned as well, arrogating to himself a Judgment which should be left to Heaven'[21], or again '*He* it must

75

be who decides the issue of Claudius' salvation, saving him for a more damnable occasion'[22]. It is a perspective accompanied appropriately by emphasis on the larger irony in the scene which shows Claudius to be not 'fit and seasoned for his passage' as he appears, but as suitable for damnation as ever.

Thus, while some have emphasized that revenge is inappropriate and ironic because inhumane in the circumstances, others have stressed that the circumstances are the fittest for revenge, making the opposite thought that revenge is inappropriate, because insufficiently horrid, ironic. With penetration and synthesis, Harry Levin has brought these conflicting, apparently irreconcilable interpretations together. He does this not without overlooking the fact that they imply opposite valuations (based on different levels of reasons) and lead to opposite conclusions about the immediate appropriateness of revenge. What permits him to overlook these, however, is his assumption that revenge is intrinsically inappropriate in any circumstances:

> For all these criticisms, on varying levels, the common stumbling block is the code of revenge, the cult of blood for blood, the incongruity of a civilized man carrying out so barbaric an imperative, flouting the laws of God and man by taking his enemy's punishment into his own hands.[23]

The convenience of Levin's synthesis for my purpose is that it shows what can become of the controversy attached to the prayer-scene when it is approached from a more comprehensive perspective. It should be clear from the point of view expressed in this study, however, that I believe Levin's perspective to be the wrong one. My own reading of the play leads me to approach the scene from the *opposite* perspective that revenge, in a strict sense, is entirely appropriate, that what is appropriate, in fact, is the right revenge. Ultimately, this leads me to see in this scene 'incongruity' of another order altogether.

To claim that Hamlet is overreaching himself and expressing hubris in the prayer-scene is to imply that Hamlet means what he says. However, it is precisely an indication of the complexity of the perspective in the scene that what Hamlet says is simultaneously a baffled substitute for what escapes him. This ambiguous quality in Hamlet's speech arises from the fact that the horridness Hamlet projects is and is not the 'horridness' Hamlet seeks, expressing Hamlet's double disposition towards an ideal and an immediate revenge. To the extent that the horridness Hamlet projects aims genuinely at the horridness Hamlet seeks (from an immediate sense of the ideal) then Hamlet means what he says, and he is expressing hubris: he is, at least, prepared to *consider* acting on something so horribly imperfect. To the extent that the projected horridness is obviously a *perversion* of the horridness sought (exposing the 'distance' of the immediate from the ideal) then Hamlet cannot mean what he says: Hamlet's projection is merely a baffled substitute for that right revenge which continues to elude him; it is clearly predicated on the knowledge that he is not *immediately* committed to act on what he says. To claim that Hamlet is not prepared to act on his projection of a more horrid fate for Claudius here might seem to be contradicted by evidence elsewhere that Hamlet *is* prepared to act on a possibility which is at least *not* the ideal act he seeks, as when Hamlet first enters in on Claudius. Yet here again Hamlet both is and is not prepared to execute his intention. To the extent that he seeks an immediate revenge, he is; to the extent that the revenge required is the ideal revenge, he is not. The emphasis when Hamlet enters, significantly, is on the nature of the possibility immediately presented as a finality (*'Now* might I do it pat, *now* 'a is a-praying; /And *now* I'll do't' (III.iii.73-74)), the question implied being: would such a revenge, seen as an accomplished act, serve? 'No', for the complex 'reasons' Hamlet gives.

Indeed, the profound ambiguity in Hamlet's disposition in this scene — an ambiguity rooted ultimately in the baffling *incongruity* of his situation — is one which Shakespeare seems almost artificially to manipulate to measure the problematic 'distance' from the ideal revenge of the revenge actually within Hamlet's grasp. It is an indication of the most complex purpose and meaning of the prayer-scene that it has been almost artifically designed to exhibit the possibilities of revenge in fact by deliberately keeping revenge *out* of Hamlet's reach. The reason for this, finally, seems to be a tactical one. Had Claudius not appeared to be doing exactly what would keep Hamlet from revenge, had Claudius, that is, not been praying, or had Hamlet at least known that Claudius was praying unsuccessfully, Hamlet would have been forced to commit himself one way or the other, and so the problematic equilibrium established in the play between the double need for an immediate and for an ideal revenge would have been destroyed. More importantly, perhaps, the play would have denied itself the opportunity of capturing this equilibrium (before the question was finally settled, as it is) in one intensely visual moment illuminating, as it were, the full import of Hamlet's predicament, as P. Alexander, *Shakespeare's Life and Art*: 'Here Shakespeare has reduced almost to visual terms the whole of Hamlet's problem.'[24] I have claimed that there is something artificial about the *way* this equilibrium is framed. More important, I believe, is the naturalness of the action itself which does not overwork the ideal revenge but makes the revenge ambiguously meditated a direct expression of the fact that Hamlet is merely in half-conscious possession of his designs, corresponding to the obliqueness with which the play is finally forced to present the ideal revenge. Ultimately, this obliqueness serves to measure the immediate possibilities of revenge for Hamlet, specifically his problematic distance from an ideal which makes all revenge properly within his grasp ultimately merely the roughest expression of the right revenge.

IV

Death

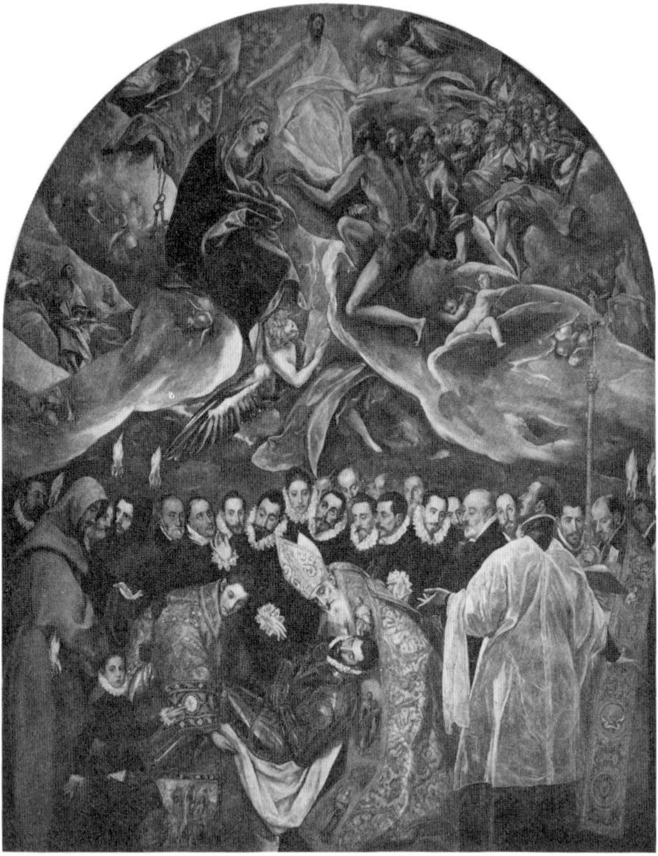

The perception of a complex operation of meaning is required to show how and in what sense the play's extended meditation on death serves in the last part of the play as a formal acknowledgment of human limitation before the mystery of visionary destiny. Here we may note to begin that the pattern of death so prominent in the last part of the play establishes itself by association with the failure of revenge, so that Hamlet's failure to act out his revenge between the prayer — and closet — scenes is immediately embodied in the death of Polonius, which may be taken in turn to stand effectively for the death of Hamlet himself, since the one leads directly to arrangements for (and formal acknowledgment of) the other (see IV.iii.65).

It is the effect of Polonius' death, moreover, to shift the burden of a father's murder from Hamlet to Laertes and Ophelia who, thus, become an immediate reflection of Hamlet's experience, but through a structure of association emphasizing Polonius' death as a literal *perpetuation* of the death of Hamlet's father in the sense that one follows directly from the failure to revenge the other. The association of all three deaths (of Polonius' death with the imminent death of Hamlet on one level of suggestion, and of these with the elder Hamlet's on another) is developed in the following climactic passage where it is also connected with the frustration and neutralization of Hamlet's revenge brought about by Hamlet's removal of himself from the scene:

O Gertrude, Gertrude!
When sorrows come, they come not single spies,
But in battalions! First, her [Ophelia's] father slain;
Next, your son gone, and he most violent author
Of his own just remove; the people muddied,
Thick and unwholesome in their thoughts and
    whispers
For good Polonius' death; and we have done but
    greenly
In hugger-mugger to inter him; poor Ophelia
Divided from herself and her fair judgment,
Without the which we are pictures, or mere beasts;
Last, and as much containing as all these,
Her brother is in secret come from France;
Feeds on his wonder, *keeps himself in clouds,*
And *wants not* buzzers *to infect his ear*
With pestilent speeches of his father's death;
Wherein necessity, of matter beggar'd,
Will nothing stick our person to arraign
In ear and ear. O my dear Gertrude, this,
Like to *a murd'ring piece*, in many places
Gives me superfluous death.

(IV.v.74-93)

The passage serves primarily to sum up for
Claudius the full extent of the harm and confusion generated by Polonius' death, harm and
confusion giving the sense of 'superfluous death'.
But the terms of the account develop simultaneously a system of suggestion associating the
'hugger-mugger' of Polonius' death with the
'hugger-mugger' involved in the interment of the
elder Hamlet, just as Laertes' clouded absorption
in rumours is associated by implication with Hamlet's clouded absorption in the revelations of the
Ghost, and the madness of Ophelia (most obvi-

ously) with Hamlet's own madness. Indeed, the full effect of the passage is to trace the developments associated with Polonius' death (developments which themselves involve the imminent death of Hamlet) implicitly back to their original source (and model) — to the developments associated with the death of the elder Hamlet. These are developments which exist primarily as an account of Hamlet's failure to revenge (traced here to conditions of clouded knowledge, self-division and errant violence) and, thus, as an account of the insidious sway and influence of 'superfluous death' in a sense unintended by Claudius, 'superfluous' in that what will be involved is an excessive number of deaths but due to an excess *unmasterableness* about the death of the elder Hamlet which makes death *intrinsically* 'superfluous'. The whole development leads to the terrible 'feast' of death at the end of the play (see V.ii.356-359) marking death's final triumph over all efforts to bring it within the possession of human power.

It is the express function of Ophelia within this larger structural development to recapitulate Hamlet's experience in its aspect of grief: 'this is the poison of deep grief' (IV.v.72). At this point, the play harks back to its more esoteric speculations on the reaches of passion. The effect of Ophelia's disjointed speech in madness is to express a fundamental incoherence of experience and expression, one which in elaborating the play's equation between shapelessness and essence (as in Hamlet's projection around the Player's performance) re-invokes the sense of void at the heart of passion.[1] Yet the void is one paradoxically challenging, by its competing intelligibility, the effort to give the essential passion shape and form, the futility of which is what can be said to account for the full pathos of the episode. Thus, 'Her speech is nothing' (IV.v.7), yet 'This nothing's more than matter' (IV.v.171), 'Though nothing sure, yet much unhappily' (IV.v.13).

In a later sequence, Laertes provides a fuller, psychological account of Ophelia's madness in grief:

> Nature is fine in love; and where 'tis fine
> It sends some precious instance of itself
> After the thing it loves.

(IV.v.158-160)

The mental strain in Ophelia's passion is specifically characterized here as an imaginative compulsion to follow after her dead father, Ophelia's passion being thus made a feature of Ophelia's psychological attempt to 'pass from nature to eternity'. It is an account which for the moment counters the essential futility of such a compulsion, sensed elsewhere in the play, with an expression of confidence in the power of emotional subtlety. As such, it develops further the analogy with Hamlet whose own grief, like Ophelia's, is what led him at first to seek for *his* dead father, at first with an extraordinary success fully bearing out such confidence in emotional subtlety, only to find that the apparent success was *really* only an extension of failure since in successfully penetrating beyond the grave to the vision of his father's Ghost, Hamlet only makes us more intensely aware of the essential gap separating him from the otherworld and the actual basis of its judgment, once that vision has faded.

By the time of the Ophelia episode, the metaphysical-psychological pattern in question has been significantly sentimentalized, even prettified, expressing the play's general modulation into pathos at this point. The sentimental reduction is explicitly acknowledged in another significant commentary of Laertes':

> Thought and affliction, passion, hell itself,
> She turns to favour and to prettiness.

(IV.v.184-185)

Here, the sentimental reconciliation of psychological tension in Ophelia reflects pathetically Hamlet's larger heroic effort to breed order out of tragic passion. Such an effort has been elaborated by the play as the attempt to assert mastery over supernatural horror, and the feature is duly reflected in the passage in the association of afflicted passion with hell. The sentimental development is brought to a climax in the Queen's speech announcing Ophelia's death (IV.vii.167-185): at this point, it is elaborated for all it has and then deflated as Ophelia is described being 'Pull'd'... 'from her melodious lay/To muddy death.' The deflation does not, however, represent complete rejection, for while the weakness of the sentimental solution is duly acknowledged, it has served to symbolize the play's contemplation of an ideal mastery over tragic passion.

Something of this function survives even the placing of the play's sentimentalism in the Clown's opening remarks in the churchyard-scene. Here, in a comic development fully expressing the play's resistance to sentimentalism, the moral incongruity of Ophelia's death is developed with all the tough impersonality of wit, as one Clown demands of the other:

> Is she to be buried in Christian burial when she wilfully seeks her own salvation?

> (v.i.1-2)

The full power of these lines lies in opposing moral incongruity to the suggestion of profounder imaginative purpose behind Ophelia's tragic sentimentalism, one ultimately linking it to Hamlet's tragic heroism; for if Ophelia can be said to have 'wilfully' sought 'salvation' through her death, it is not merely in a purely ironic sense emphasizing moral violation. The action symbolizes, at the same time, through an equation of full metaphysical mastery with salvation, the imaginative effort to achieve full metaphysical mastery over tragic passion. Since it is in the nature of such passion in the play's terms to be subject to the dissociation of death (what separates 'nature' from 'eternity'), the effort of mastery is seen appropriately as a wilful precipitation into death.

Such an action can be said to constitute an effort towards 'salvation' in the psychological sense, but it is an action which also involves the risk of damnation in the moral, as well as destruction in the psychological, sense. Thus, if Ophelia is said to 'seek' her own 'salvation', it is the 'salvation' which would come from a full reconciliation of moral conflict with psychological need, the basic incongruity of which is what the Clown's remarks finally serve to emphasize. Seen as such, Ophelia's fate measures Hamlet's own fuller, psychological-heroic 'struggle' with death and damnation: the value of Ophelia's fate is that it confidently acts out on one level what Hamlet himself falls short of on another, due to his scepticism. That scepticism is also the play's, and it is expressed again with Ophelia through the Clown and then in the Priest's judgment over Ophelia's burial:

> Her death was doubtful;
> And, but that great command o'ersways the order,
> She should in ground unsanctified have lodg'd
> Till the last trumpet...

(V.i.221-224)

Here, however, that scepticism is balanced with an expression of confidence in the integrity of Ophelia's purpose, and a claim to the reversibility of the moral judgment; thus Laertes:

> I tell thee, churlish priest,
> A minist'ring angel shall my sister be
> When thou liest howling...

(V.i.234-236)

89

This brief account of the Ophelia episode should be enough to hint at the complexity of the dramatic development in this part of the play. Our sense of the episode's dramatic power stems from our experience of the tension between levels of meaning, between what might be called the episode's sentimental and symbolical functions. A similarly rich suggestiveness is developed round the figure of Laertes, whose dramatic power in this part of the play stems likewise from a tension between functions, though here the application is different. In the Ophelia episode, the sentimental reduction which the episode can be said to enact is what permits the full, unhampered symbolic exploration of visionary destiny. It is because the play already recognizes that the sentimental solution in Ophelia's experience could not by itself apply to Hamlet without serious reduction, that the play can permit itself a full exploration of the solution while avoiding inappropriate encroachment. By contrast, in the Laertes episode, similar recognition of a fundamental reduction in the comparison of Laertes' experience with Hamlet's is what makes the unqualified encroachment on Hamlet of the *melodramatic* solution in Laertes' experience maddeningly inappropriate, all the more so because the encroachment is so plausible and inevitable. The different application is used to different ends, expressing subtly varied perspectives on the control of visionary destiny. The purpose of the Ophelia episode is to outline within a given recognition of failure, the possibility of success; the purpose of the Laertes episode to re-enact, within an outline of success, the full frustration of failure.

Laertes' encroachment on Hamlet is formally developed at IV.vii, when Claudius, showing a typical political cunning no less formidable for being coldly sinister, succeeds masterfully in absorbing Laertes' obsession with revenge into the swordfight-plot. He does this mainly by dwelling on the envy caused to Hamlet by the special praise given to Laertes for his qualities of swordsmanship by the mysterious Norman, Lamord. Claudius' carefully measured broaching of Laertes' reputation does not merely serve an ironic purpose: the extolment is not merely meant to point up, by contrast, all that makes Laertes' obviously shallow heroism so decidedly inferior to Hamlet's. The shallowness of this heroism is pronounced, and it is brought out marvellously through the skilful manner with which Claudius exploits Laertes' quiet but obvious vulnerability to praise, thus achieving the breakdown of Laertes' purpose. However, Claudius' extolment serves at the same time to build up the genuine encroachment of Laertes' heroism on Hamlet's, a development remarkable for taking place simultaneously with the breakdown and reduction just described. It is all the more remarkable as a development in being unaided by any previous suggestion, for being carried purely through the extolment itself, which succeeds due to the gratuitous prestige thrown over it by the mysterious associations of Lamord.

The purpose of Laertes' encroachment on Hamlet is to prepare for and build up a fundamental rivalry between the two, the significance of which is not made fully clear until the formal struggle between Laertes and Hamlet in Ophelia's grave, when encroachment and rivalry are brought to a climax couching the explanation. Of this confrontation Hamlet says later 'the bravery of his grief did put me/Into a tow'ring passion' (V.ii.79-80). However, the straightforwardness of Hamlet's explanation in fact obscures the deeper import attached to it. Hamlet is stirred to outburst partly, as he remarks, over the offensiveness of Laertes' melodramatic heroism. What makes this heroism offensive is the ease with which it is in part assumed and aimed at Hamlet as a judgment on him for Ophelia's death. What it undermines is the crucial part played in this death by the larger struggle that has kept Hamlet from acting on such heroism in his own pursuit of revenge precisely from his commitment to a deeper, genuinely visionary heroism. The deeper irony, however, is that the heroism which Laertes himself so uncritically assumes, the heroism for which Hamlet is shown elsewhere to have such inevitable contempt, is the only heroism of which Hamlet himself is ever seen to be *fully* capable. It is entirely to the point here that Hamlet should be driven by Laertes' heroism not to the expression of a more genuine heroism but merely to a more intense expression of the same, making us poignantly aware of the deeper, visionary heroism that has *escaped* Hamlet, our sense of which reduces his own immediate expression of heroism here to the level of 'rant' (V.i.278). The association of Hamlet's heroism with Laertes' is fully suggested at Hamlet's formal entrance onto the scene, in the ambiguity of his address which leaves it unclear at first whether by the 'emphasis' of grief (V.i.249) Hamlet has in mind Laertes' struggle *or his own*:

> What is he whose grief
> Bears such an emphasis, whose phrase of sorrow
> Conjures the wand'ring stars, and makes them stand
> Like wonder-wounded hearers? This is I,
> Hamlet the Dane.

(V.i.248-252)

It is thus that the encroachment of Laertes on Hamlet is achieved. Hamlet's outrage in this scene stems from his sense of the fundamental reduction implied in the encroachment of Laertes' heroism on his own. That outrage is made all the more urgent and intense by the full plausibility of the encroachment, from the failure of heroism that has made a superficial comparison of Laertes' with his own inevitable. The purpose of Laertes' encroachment is to re-enact for Hamlet the full frustration of failure: it is the occasion of a struggle that is as much Hamlet's struggle to free himself from a real enslavement to a melodramatic heroism as it is his struggle to assert to the world that his own heroism is greater and harder than a purely melodramatic heroism. This 'struggle' takes place appropriately in the grave:

> Dost come here to whine?
> To outface me with leaping in her grave?
> Be buried quick with her, and so will I.

(V.i.271-273)

thus bringing to dramatic definition the play's association of an incomplete mastery over visionary destiny with the impenetrability of death, here ultimately a measure of its 'superfluity'. Hamlet's failure to revenge is to be traced ultimately to the impenetrability of his father's death, specifically to Hamlet's clouded knowledge of the otherworld which has made full mastery of visionary judgment impossible. Similarly the incomplete mastery of such judgment seen as an ironic struggle against the melodramatic reduction, is associated here with the *futility* of a literal confrontation with death (the melodramatic reduction being ultimately a measure of the limitations that prevent full power over death).

The limiting factor in Hamlet's experience which we know elsewhere to be his inability to penetrate once again beyond the grave into a full vision of the otherworld is thus seen to be the tyranny of the grave poignantly focused here in Ophelia's corpse which is all that survives of *her* precipitation into death, just as all that can be said to survive of Hamlet's own penetration beyond death to the vision of his dead father ultimately is the vivid memory of his father's 'dead corse'

(I.iv.52) 'cast up' (51) from the grave. The power which Hamlet requires in order to achieve full mastery over his destiny is the power which the play reserves for the mysterious Lamord who, as his name implies, is Death itself: the power to be 'incorps'd' (IV.vii.87), with all that this projects of full possession and knowledge of death and thus, in the play's terms, full possession and knowledge of the otherworld. It is a power which the play associates in the Lamord passage (IV.vii.84-92) with a power of metamorphosis, with a symbolical unification in horsemanship of horseman with horse, terms set by the ultimately chivalric import of Hamlet's struggle with Laertes (and all that he represents about Hamlet) in the face of Death. Whether or not Hamlet can be said in this struggle ultimately to attain to a full power over Death or a power approaching Death, or even to unite himself to Death is a question that seems predetermined by the associations of futility attached to Hamlet's struggle in the grave. But in fact all such associations are further subordinated to a significant reduction of the struggle involved in Hamlet's formal renunciation of the struggle later as implied in his apology to Laertes at V.ii.218-236. The effect of this reduction is to turn the use the play makes of Lamord as a symbolical heightening of the struggle with Death into a purely isolated phenomenon which significantly the play ultimately fails to develop.

Yet, if the play cannot in the end permit itself any suggestion of full triumph over death or even of a struggle challenging triumph, it seems eager to elaborate evidence of a 'return' from death, of providential immunity from the premature death that would mean complete frustration of revenge and the final perpetuation of injustice. Crucial to this development is the full import of Hamlet's experience at sea, which, as Hamlet's note to Claudius duly records, has been the 'occasion' of his 'sudden and more strange return' (IV.vii.46-47). Return from what, Hamlet's remarks in his letter to Horatio make clear: if Hamlet exhorts Horatio to 'repair' to him 'with as much speed as he wouldst fly death' (IV.vi.20-21), that is because Hamlet's experience has been for him a 'return' from death, the 'bore of the matter' (23), being that Hamlet is providentially snatched up just when death seemed inevitable (while, by contrast, Rosencrantz and Guildenstern themselves go to their own deaths when least expecting it, in the full irony of such ignorance as Hamlet might have fallen victim to himself). The pattern of 'return' which Hamlet's fate finally demonstrates is no isolated development: it represents the dramatic turning-point in the pattern of 'return' which the whole play can be said to enact in demonstrating how the final revenge is achieved through the succession of 'purposes mistook/Fall'n on th' inventors' heads' (V.ii.376-377). The significance of this very elaborate pattern is that it balances the play's portrayal of Hamlet's failure up to that point with the compensating perception of a guiding providence working directly through failure, indeed in the case of the conflict between

Hamlet and Claudius, through different orders of limitations which ensure, by the 'return' from death which both experience, the inevitable and independent operation of divine justice.

Claudius is himself unable to profit fully from the death of the elder Hamlet, from limitations which ensure that murder shall always be exposed, even, if necessary, through extraordinary means, for example, through the revelation of a ghost; and just as Hamlet is unable for his part to arrange for the death of Claudius from the limitations which prevent him from framing Claudius' death within a totally actual realization of otherworldly judgment, so too Claudius is unable in his turn to arrange for the death of Hamlet, at first from the more mundane limitations that prevent him from pronouncing sentence on Hamlet for Polonius' death from fear of public outrage, limitations seen implicitly as an extension of the limitations besetting Hamlet ('And where 'tis so, the offender's scourge is weigh'd,/But never the offence', (IV.iii.6-7)); then, from the limitations that prevent Claudius from securing Hamlet's death in England due to a shaping divinity which represents as much a mockery of Hamlet's own ponderous plotting as it is more obviously a frustration of Claudius'.

It is the function of the play's catastrophe to bring to a dramatic climax Hamlet's hard-won faith in a guiding providence at work independently in developments in his world. It is indeed as the fruit and end-product of a very extensive ef-

fort to penetrate imaginatively to the inner determination of phenomenal developments in the
world (a motivation that the graveyard meditation
suggests dies hard) that we must view the suggestion to Horatio, after the adventure at sea, that
behind the world's pattern of developments Hamlet has seen the operation of a shaping hand
working directly *through* frustration of the visionary struggle:

> let us know,
> Our indiscretion sometimes serves us well,
> When our deep plots do pall; and that should learn us
> There's a divinity that shapes our ends,
> Rough-hew them how we will.

(V.ii.7-11)

It is the climax to that general condition in Hamlet throughout the play which shows him, despite
the sincerity of his commitment to revenge,
progressively absorbed in the drift of the world,
involved through his dealings with the Court,
apparently unnecessarily, at first with the Players,
then with Fortinbras' army, and, later still, in the
adventure at sea, and the swordfight with Laertes.
The strength of Hamlet's perception with Horatio
derives from the fact that it is rooted deeply in
Hamlet's experience in this regard, when Hamlet's
visionary struggle —having by the time of the sea
adventure come to great impasse

> ...in my heart there was a kind of fighting

(V.ii.4)

— gives way, by a mysterious transformation, to the drive which lifts Hamlet providentially out of his despair. Despair of the visionary struggle is now compensated for by the self-transforming discovery of *integrity* in the disposition of events, saving Hamlet from premature death, and returning him to Denmark. Although it is part of the effect of this discovery to leave Hamlet still buoyed in the confidence of an inevitable rendering of judgment, this judgment is now felt to be independent of his own determination; in fact, it is immediately accompanied by an *intensification* of the possible prospect of his own death and the related acceptance of the very large risk this prospect involves of a possible reprieve and lease on life for Claudius the malefactor.

Hamlet's discovery, paradoxically, is of *integrity* in this pattern. It is because the reversal at sea saves Hamlet from a course leading directly to his own death — because the reversal operates from deep within the pattern of failure — that an expectation of ultimate providence is engendered in Hamlet strong enough to justify renewed appearances of waywardness when Hamlet willingly submits himself later on to suspicions of a new threat on his life and the renewed prospect of failure represented by the swordfight with Laertes. It is an expectation that comes to be linked with an attitude of resignation in Hamlet before an experience of Providence thought by some to represent a profound religious feeling, by others the fatalism of a *gran rifiuto*. It does not require any elaborate defense of structural complexity to realize that it is a measure of both. Hamlet's feeling is in fact the more intense for this, for, genuinely and profoundly religious as it is, it is a feeling that asserts itself finally in direct relation to *failure* by the standards of the visionary struggle that has involved Hamlet throughout the play. Indeed, it is a feeling difficult for Hamlet to sustain in the balance of truth that yet continues to press in on him. Or at least a sense of reality at once larger and less assuring than the positive security of religious feeling must be invoked to account for the very complex mood ultimately associated with Hamlet's feeling, where strains of pathos and irony finally mingle uneasily with the faith expressed:

HAM.: But thou wouldst not think how ill all's here about my heart; but it is no matter.

HOR.: Nay, good my lord —

HAM.: It is but foolery; but it is such a kind of gaingiving as would perhaps trouble a woman.

HOR.: If your mind dislike anything, obey it. I will forestall their repair hither, and say you are not fit.

HAM.: Not a whit, we defy augury: there is a special providence in the fall of a sparrow. If it be now, 'tis not to come; if it be not to come, it will be now; if it be not now, yet it will come — the readiness is all. Since no man owes of aught he leaves, what is't to leave betimes? Let be.

(V.ii.203ff)

Walker is no doubt right too in suggesting that we are ultimately meant to view the image of a divinity that shapes our ends in the 'readiness'

Hamlet brings to the swordfight with Laertes.[2] Yet we must bring to bear on this account a further crucial observation: the image we are left with in the end, an image otherwise associated with action built up on a tremendous scale, is an image nonetheless radically undevelopped as an elucidation of the workings of Providence. It recalls, in this respect, a similar absence of development of the Death-impinging qualities associated through Lamord with the chivalric struggle between Laertes and Hamlet. The reduction of theme which both omissions imply can be seen operating in the reversal through which the resolution of the action is secured: 'Laertes wounds Hamlet: then in scuffling, they change rapiers, and Hamlet wounds Laertes.' That chivalry which in the Lamord passage had been transformed into the image of Death becomes in the collapse of struggle into scuffle, something considerably removed from such an image, being reduced to something far less than chivalry. The disposition of the outcome can be said to be achieved, likewise, through a reversal that substitutes, for the image of triumphant Providence one had been led to expect of such an action, merely the predominance of superior physical strength and energy. The treatment points to a deliberate reduction of theme which is total: human action is stripped of any of the larger, metaphysical associations that might be developed round it, as if Shakespeare himself retreated from a final penetration of such associations.

The reduction which the action undergoes in the last part of the play is one also applied to the play's central focus on the possibility of visionary development. What we must recognize in considering the full significance of the final action is the overadded awareness which we bring to the catastrophe from the play's previous visionary tenor, an awareness which compels us to see in the play's resolution ultimately merely the faintest echo of the elusive *visionary* resolution previously associated with the full implications of the action. E.E. Stoll has brought attention to the 'crowded and explosive' nature of the catastrophe, which finds its 'outward and sensuous emphasis' in the dramatic use of artillery:

these thunders break out properly enough (on a stage where such portentous noise was not uncommon or illegitimate) not only to mark and distinguish the palpable hits in the fencing match, but, both there and after the eulogy, to signalize the importance of the scene as a whole. Where emotional effect is the chief concern, a greater weight of emphasis is, as in music, indispensable.[3]

Yet it seems obvious that no amount of emphasis *in this kind* could ever be powerful enough to distract us sufficiently from the full, metaphysical emphasis one *might* have expected of the catastrophe from major developments in the play. Here we may note specifically that no amount of thunderous 'bruiting' between the heavens and the earth (I.ii.127; V.ii.267-269) could ever substitute for the visionary-judgmental thun-

dering this may be taken to suggest, any more
than the purely verbal intensity of Hamlet's emotional rant earlier could have been mistaken for
the visionary 'horrid speech':

> What would he do,
> Had he the motive and the cue for passion
> That I have? He would drown the stage with tears,
> And cleave the general ear with horrid speech;
>
> ....
>   amaze indeed
> The very faculties of eyes and ears.
>
> ....
>   Bloody, bawdy villain!
> Remorseless, treacherous, lecherous kindless villain!
> O, vengeance!
>
> (II.ii.553ff)

And as with the general effect of the catastrophe, so too with Hamlet's moment of revenge:

> Here, thou incestuous, murd'rous, damned Dane,
> Drink off this potion. Is thy union here?
> Follow my mother.
>
> (V.ii.317-319)

Powerful as this is on its own level, it focuses
the supernatural consequences of the union in the
otherworld in such a manner as to suggest the
dramatic borderline separating imminent judgment beyond death from the full, immediate vision of such judgment from this side of the world.
The latter, I believe, is the kind of knowledge
which the play has envisaged for Hamlet from the
first, although it is the kind of knowledge which
always remains significantly *beyond* the reach of
the action. Indeed, this is also part of the poign-

ant effect of the vision of choiring angels which Horatio projects as attending the progress of Hamlet's soul beyond death, as if pointing us again to that visionary realm lying just beyond the play's action:

> Good night, sweet prince,
> And flights of angels sing thee to thy rest!

(V.ii.350-351)

The stringent exploration of visionary possibility provided over the course of the play will have persuaded us of a standpoint too disturbingly problematic for us to be easily convinced of the immediate relevance to Hamlet's experience of such a visionary idea as Horatio innocently projects around Hamlet, in the spirit of *one* experience of the Renaissance visionary ideal as one finds this represented, for example, in El Greco.[4] And yet, it is equally true that one does not feel at the play's close that Horatio's eulogy might not still properly apply to Hamlet, even as we have known him implicated in tragedy. Indeed, one seems bound to acknowledge that it might yet be in the nature of the profoundly paradoxical development towards religious reconciliation in this last part of the play to admit of such a determination of fate for Hamlet in spite of the quite emphatically problematic value of Hamlet's action right up to the time of his death. In fact, I would go so far as to claim that a projection of a visionary destiny that is final and unproblematic is assumed in Hamlet all along as motivating inspiration and ideal. By the end this is an ideal that has been very significantly frustrated and undermined as a basis for action, but for all this, it is an ideal that we may *yet* be meant to suppose maintained and observed in Hamlet, insofar as the psychological tragedy is consistently *resisted* in him, in spite of the many deaths he has caused by the end. The ideal is, in any case, boldly set off and released at the end as from a long and difficult gestation. And Hamlet might yet be allowed to die in an inheritance of it. But, if so, only by a difficult paradoxical determination over which Shakespeare has become by then himself problematically silent, having become in the end of *Hamlet* metaphysically disengaged.

Notes

Preface

1. John Dillenberger, ed., *Martin Luther: Selections from His Writings* (New York: Doubleday, 1961), p. xxviii.
2. For a close account of the many parallels between the action in Hamlet and Luther's life and thought, see the recent article by Raymond Waddington in *English Language Notes*, Volume XXVII, No. 2, 1989, pp. 27-42.
3. Martin Luther, 'Preface to the Complete Edition of Luther's Latin Writings', from *Martin Luther,* ed., Dillenberger, p. 11.
4. Ibid., p. 11.
5. Dillenberger, *Martin Luther,* p. xxix.
6. Ibid., p. xxix.

I
Sorrow

1. All quotations are taken from the edition by Lily B. Campbell, ed., *The Mirror for Magistrates* (Cambridge: Cambridge University Press, 1938).
2. See Alwin Thaler, 'Literary Criticism in *A Mirror for Magistrates*', *JEGP* 49, 1950, no.1.
3. See John Lydgate, *The Fall of Princes*, ed., Henry Bergen (London: Oxford University Press, 1967), Book I, l.477, p. 14.
4. Howard Baker, *Induction to Tragedy* (Louisiana: Louisiana State University Press, 1939), p. 111.
5. Thomas Kyd, *The Spanish Tragedy*, ed. Philip Edwards (London: Metheun, 1959; rpt., 1973).
6. From 'The Theme of Damnation in Dr. Faustus', *Marlowe: Doctor Faustus: A Casebook*, ed., John Jump (London: Macmillan, 1969), p. 95.

7. See 'Appendix I', scene xii, from the Revels edition ed. John Jump (London: Methuen, 1962), pp. 115-116. The fact that the Emperor's speech belongs to the 1604 A-text of Marlowe's play, which is no longer regarded, and has not been for some time, as the authoritative text — the A-text having been judged by Greg (originally) to be a memorial reconstruction by actors of the original prompt-book for provincial performance — this, it would seem, decisive fact does not at all detract from my argument here insofar as the very supposition of a speech in these terms, as such evidence suggests, by someone not Marlowe, merely lends support to my claim about a general Renaissance concern.

8. All references are to the Alexander Text (London: Collins, 1951).

9. See *The Time Is Out of Joint* (London: Andrew Dakers, 1948), p. 28.

10. See G.K. Hunter, *Dramatic Identities and Cultural Tradition* (Liverpool: Liverpool University Press, 1978).

11. Classical mythology only gives evidence of an uninterrupted egress through the gates, and from this point of view, Kyd's action represents a dramatic break with tradition. Kyd's innovation, however, corresponds strictly to his ultimate theme which, as I show below, has to do with man's tragic separation from an otherworldly experience.

Kyd frankly assumes the existence of the otherworld, but what he wishes to dramatize is the tragic realization that man no longer has available to him *full* consciousness of an otherworldly experience. Hence, the disruption in Andrea's visionary journey, which is not as it may appear, a matter of ingress after egress, but rather of *aborted* egress or the sudden deflation of vision. Hunter's view that the egress is into the world of the play leaves us with the entirely meaningless assumption that the 'reality' corresponding to

the 'dream' of the play is the otherworld from which
Andrea has come, an otherworld of which Andrea tells
us that he himself has had but an aborted glimpse.
What, in that case, would be the significance of the
'reality' of the audience would drive us into yet deeper
spheres of metaphysical obnubilation.

In any case, the otherworld is traditionally the
locus of the dream-vision.

12. For an extensive consideration of dream-vision literature up to the reign of Henry VIII, see A.C. Spear-
ing, *Medieval Dream Poetry* (Cambridge, 1976). As for
the Elizabethans, it would take Shakespeare, with his
acute sense of its dramatic possibilities, to revitalize
this material to greatest effect — as in Clarence's
dream from *Richard III*, where the dream-vision structure merges with the material of the marvellous journey into hell (with its echo of Kyd) to serve the
projection of a powerful representation of the revolted
fate of tragic guilt:

No, no, my dream was lengthen'd after life.
O, then began the tempest to my soul!
I pass'd, methought, the melancholy flood
With that sour ferryman which poets write of,
Unto the kingdom of perpetual night.
The first that there did greet my stranger soul
Was my great father-in-law, renowned Warwick,
Who spoke aloud 'What scourge for perjury
Can this dark monarchy afford false Clarence?'
And so he vanish'd. Then came wand'ring by
A shadow like an angel, with bright hair
Dabbled in blood, and he shriek'd out aloud
'Clarence is come — false, fleeting, perjur'd
    Clarence,
That stabb'd me in the field by Tewksbury.
Seize on him, Furies, take him unto torment!
With that, methoughts, a legion of foul fiends
Environ'd me, and howled in mine ears.

109

Such hideous cries that, with that very noise,
I trembling wak'd, and for a season after
Could not believe but that I was in hell,
Such terrible impression made my dream.

(I.iv.43-63)

II
Sexuality

1. Opp. exeg. lat., I, 212, 26-27, 29-30 1536 *Weim*; LXII,
8-10; cited by Hiram Haydn, *The Counter-Renaissance*
(New York: Harcourt, Brace and World Inc., 1950),
p. 417.

2. See Nicholas Brooke, *Shakespeare's Early Tragedies*
(London: Methuen, 1968), p. 186.

3. See E.M.W. Tillyard, *Shakespeare's Problem Plays*
(Toronto: Toronto University Press, 1950), p.24.

III
Revenge

1. See D.G. James, *The Dream of Learning* (London:
Oxford at the Clarendon Press, 1951), particularly
pp.38-43; Arthur Sewell, *Character and Society in
Shakespeare* (Oxford: Clarendon Press, 1951), p. 77;
Douglas Bush, *Shakespeare and the Natural Condition*
(Cambridge, Mass.: Harvard University Press, 1956),
particularly pp. 83-84.

2. See Arthur Sewell, *Character and Society*, p. 77.

3. See A.W. Von Schlegal, from *Dramatic Art and Lit-
erature*, 1809-1811, as quoted by A.C. Bradley,
Shakespearean Tragedy (London: Macmillan, Student
Editions, 1974; orig. pub., 1904), p. 83; S.T. Coleridge,
Coleridge on Shakespeare, ed. Terence Hawkes
(Harmondsworth: Penguin Books, 1969), p. 174;
Edward Dowden, *Shakspere: His Mind and Art* (Lon-

don: Kegan Paul, Trench, Trubner, 1892), p. 133. For a modern re-statement of this position, see H.B. Charlton, *Shakespearian Tragedy* (Cambridge: Cambridge University Press, 1948; rpt. Norwich: Jarrold & Sons, 1952), p. 93. For an eloquent *attack* freeing Hamlet from the charge of irresolution, see A.C. Swinburne, *A Study of Shakespeare* (London: William Heinemann, 1920; first pub., Chatto and Windus, 1879), pp. 168-169.

4. See Patrick Cruttwell, 'The Morality of *Hamlet*: "Sweet Prince or Arrant Knave'?' from *Hamlet*, ed., J.R. Brown and Bernard Harris, *Stratford-Upon-Avon Studies* 5 (London: Edward Arnold, 1963), p. 111.

5. See A.C. Bradley, *Shakespearean Tragedy*, p.79; J.D. Wilson, *What Happens in* Hamlet (London: University Press, 1935, rpt., 1962) pp. 72,84; H.D.F. Kitto, *Form and Meaning in Drama* (London: Methuen, 1956; rpt. 1964) pp. 286-287; H.B. Charlton, *Shakespearian Tragedy* (Cambridge: Cambridge University Press, 1948), pp. 86-87; and Kenneth Muir, *Shakespeare:* Hamlet (London: Edward Arnold, 1963; rpt., 1969), p. 56.

6. For emphasis on the Ghost as a symbol of fate, see I.iv.81; for manifestations of an overwhelming desire to get the Ghost to speak, see I.i. 49-51; I.i. 127-139; and particularly, I.iv.40-44, where the desire to get the Ghost to speak overrides the consideration of whether it is good or evil.

7. See J.M. Robertson, *The Problems of* Hamlet (London: George Allen Unwin Ltd., 1919), p. 74; A.J.A. Waldock, Hamlet: *A Study in Critical Method* (London: Cambridge University Press, 1931), p. 66; Helen Gardner, *The Business of Criticism* (London: Oxford at the Clarendon Press, 1959), p. 46; and Harry Levin, *The Question of* Hamlet (New York: Oxford University Press, 1959), pp. 56-57. Harold Jenkins has, in his

Arden edition of the play (London: Methuen, 1982), himself brought up this major stumbling block in the appraisal of Hamlet's predicament, with prominent allusion to L.C. Knights, *An Approach to* Hamlet, and Eleanor Prosser, *Hamlet and Revenge.*

8. See A.C. Bradley, *Shakespearean Tragedy,* p. 96: 'the demand on him, in the name of everything dearest and most sacred, to arise and act'; and G. Wilson Knight, *The Wheel of Fire* (London: Methuen, 1961; first pub., 1930), p.20; 'to cleanse, to create harmony'.

9. See particularly A.C. Bradley, p.141; and J.D. Wilson, p. 72.

10. See Levin, p. 56.

11. See Muir, *Shakespeare:* Hamlet, p. 67.

12. Levin, pp. 83-85.

13. Levin, p. 34.

14. See Gardner, p. 46; Wilson Knight, p.36.

15. See Peter Alexander, *Hamlet, Father and Son* (London: Clarendon Press, 1955), pp. 144-145; A.C. Bradley, p. 80.

16. See D.G. James, *The Dream of Learning,* pp. 45-46.

17. See Waldock, p.43.

18. See Kitto, p. 315.

19. See Maynard Mack, 'The World of Hamlet', *The Yale Review,* xli, 1951-1952, p. 508.

20. Mack, p. 522.

21. Kitto, p. 315.

22. Mack, p. 522.

23. Levin, pp. 34-35.

24. Cited by Jenkins, p. 140.

IV
Death

1. See II.ii. 548-550: 'Tears in his eyes, distraction in's aspect,/ A broken voice, and his whole function suiting/ With forms to his conceit?'

2. See Roy Walker, *The Time is Out of Joint* (London: Andrew Dakers, 1948), p.152.

3. See E.E. Stoll, *Art and Artifice in Shakespeare* (London: Methuen, 1963; orig.pub. Barnes and Noble, 1933), p.127-128.

4. See El Greco's painting *Burial of the Count of Orgaz*.

Printed by
Ateliers Graphiques Marc Veilleux Inc.
Cap-Saint-Ignace Qué.
in May 1991